Consciousness and
the Study of Society

Consciousness and the Study of Society

TOWARDS A NEW PERSPECTIVE ON SOCIOLOGY

First Edition

Charles DeMotte

SUNY – Cortland

cognella® | ACADEMIC PUBLISHING

Bassim Hamadeh, CEO and Publisher
John Remington, Executive Editor
Gem Rabanera, Senior Project Editor
Christian Berk, Production Editor
Jess Estrella, Senior Graphic Designer
Stephanie Kohl, Licensing Coordinator
Natalie Piccotti, Director of Marketing
Kassie Graves, Vice President of Editorial
Jamie Giganti, Director of Academic Publishing

Printed in the United States of America.

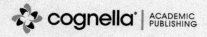

Contents

Unit II   Fundamental Ideas of the Social World

Unit III   Social Differentiations

Preface

The study of sociology assumes (quite rightly) that our lives are conditioned largely through interactions with others. If you think about it, many of our daily activities center around people, either on an individual or group basis. Such interactions are not merely responses to groups or individuals, but perceptions of the social world filtered through our consciousness. Consciousness pertains to our level of awareness, but awareness of what? Since our waking moments are often spent in the realms of memory, feeling, and thought as well as our physical situation, the social realm of our existence is far more complicated than what it might, at first, seem. While this textbook is largely concerned with the fundamentals of sociology, there is a presumption that perceptions based on one's level of consciousness shape the world in which we live, move, and have our being.

The chapters of this book are placed within five headings or categories. The first category, covering chapters 1–4, is entitled *Basic Assumptions and Analysis*. This group of chapters discusses the theoretical, analytical, and methodological groundwork for the study of sociology, including a brief consideration of the human constitution. Chapters 5–8, included under the heading of *Fundamental Ideas of the Social World*, look at the basic ideas that underscore sociology including culture, society, socialization (psychological & social learning), and how we make sense of everyday life. The section on *Social Differentiations*, Chapters 9–12, takes account of social stratification and class, race, ethnicity, gender, deviance and social control, and sexuality. In other words, issues of social identity and those factors that make certain groups distinctive and often times conflicted. The next six chapters, 13–18, deal with *Foundational Institutions* that focus on six primary social structures that are the foundational backbones of any society, including family, politics, economics, religion, education, along with health and medicine. Finally the last two chapters, 19 and 20, are included under the heading *Transitions to a New Age*. The assumption here is that the upheavals in our present society are the harbinger of a society that will be far different from our own, which in evolutionary terms represents a new cycle of human experience.

UNIT I

Basic Assumptions
and Analysis

THE FIRST FOUR chapters lay the groundwork for the rest of the book. Since sociology is fundamentally about people and their interactions, the first chapter is devoted to an investigation of self, probing the depths of who we are, which comprise different levels of consciousness both impermanent and permanent. Because we experience the world through different planes of awareness, we see our environment through the lens of perception. The sociological perception assumes that we are part of a larger society, and that our thoughts and actions are shaped and conditioned by the social world. Accordingly, there are three basic images of society, referred to as the structural-functional paradigm, the conflict paradigm, and the interactive paradigm. The validity of our perceptions is the result of an ability to think clearly. If ideas are to have any meaning, they must be based on facts (evidence) that can be verified and proved through the process of reason and logic. Hence, critical thinking is vital for ascertaining truth and discerning the real from the unreal. Critical thinking is the foundation of the scientific method, which is the basis of sociological research. Since sociology is a scientific study of society, it is important to understand the terminology and connections which underscore the scientific method, along with the methodologies and steps one must follow in doing valid research.

CHAPTER ONE

The Human Constitution

WHO ARE YOU? This is a question which confounds most people. When asked, the responses often relate to attributes of oneself such as one's name, occupation, gender, or some such thing. However, these are just labels that have no real relation to the various aspects of self. Even if we probe further, the way we see ourselves is only partial, impermanent, and essentially erroneous. In point of fact we know very little about ourselves and much less about the world around us. Physically, our bodies consist of cells, composed of atoms comprising various sub-atomic particles, which, as physics has demonstrated, are nothing more than manifestations of energy vibrations. Essentially, all that exist are energies and forces. One could, therefore, legitimately ask the question of whether we as identifiable beings exist at all, but this is beside the point. Sociology is predicated on how people interact with one another within various societies. In order to comprehend how society functions, we need to get an understanding of the energies and forces that make up the dimensions of the human constitution, so the question *"Who are you?"* can have some meaning.

CONSCIOUSNESS

The reason we have the ability to understand ourselves is because we are a conscious being. In fact, all living entities are conscious to some degree. **Consciousness** is defined as *the state of being awake and aware of one's surroundings.* Since consciousness runs through all the kingdoms of nature, we might ask how the consciousness of a human differs from that of a cat, dog, ape, or fly. To answer this question, it is important to remember that the natural world is primarily a hierarchy of classes, divisions, kingdoms, phylum, orders, families, genera, and species. Moreover, all elements of the natural world are subject to the law of evolution. **Evolution** is *the gradual development of something,*

FIGURE 1.1. The Evolution of Man.

especially from a simple to a complex form.[1] Charles Darwin and others put forth the theory that species evolve through natural selection and adaptation to their environment. This orthodox definition, however, is limited. Seemingly, consciousness is the product of evolution. If evolution is true, then it must logically apply to all living forms and, in the case of humans, to every level of one's being. In this light, human evolution is a complex process of consciousness development, not only in a physical sense, but emotionally, intellectually, and beyond. Fundamentally, consciousness is a relationship between these different components of self. If we think about who we are, it follows that the response will depend on the focus of our identity within the differing states of consciousness.

THE IMPERMANENT CHARACTERISTICS OF SELF

Returning to the question *"Who are you?"* we begin with the obvious fact that we have a physical body. The level of consciousness associated with the physical world is instinct. **Instinct** is defined as *an innate, typically fixed pattern in animals in response to certain stimuli.* If we as humans were strictly centered at this plane of awareness, we would be attuned and responsive to our immediate environment in much the same way as are the various grades of animals. While animals possess feelings, their cognitive faculties are dormant. At this stage, humans might be considered just as higher forms of animal life.

---

1   *American Heritage® Dictionary of the English Language*, 5th ed., s.v. "evolution," https://www.thefreedictionary.com/evolution.

PLATE III

1   4

2   5

3   6

FIGURE 1.2. Feelings or Emotions.

Moving on, we are also aware of having an emotional nature. The word itself, *emotion* contains a clue as to the characteristics of the emotions, namely that they are constantly in state of motion and flux driven by desire, which is a strong feeling of wanting something or the wish for something to happen. It might be said that desire is a disturbance of feeling. A **feeling is** *an emotional state or reaction*. At a basic level, our emotions vacillate between pleasure and pain. We covet food, sex, status, attention, companionship, and various possessions; at the same time, we try to avoid those things that cause us discomfort. There is a wide range of emotions but they all relate to the personal self. Experience through the emotions is gained by means of the five senses: hearing, touch, sight, taste, and smell. We can directly experience a feeling through one of our senses, but it takes the use of the mind to know that we have had that feeling, much less to explain its meaning. Therefore, sensory consciousness, or perception, is achieved through the relationship between thought and feeling derived through the senses.

Beyond our emotions, we are also aware that we have a mind. The French philosopher, René Descartes (1596–1650) is attributed with having the realization "I think therefore I am," which was his answer to the "*Who am I?*" question. Neuroscientists, psychologists, and others have maintained for years that consciousness is centered in the brain. Essentially, they are missing the wider dimension. Why is this so? An analogy can be made with the impact of media. Essentially, media consists of messages passed along a medium to a receiver. In contrast to the individualistic model that posits a direct connection between information that is sent directly to the brain and a corresponding response, an alternative model depicts the instantaneous transmission of information through a medium that so saturates the psychic atmosphere (sphere of mental activity) that it is experienced simultaneously by numerous people over a wide area. Consequently, the mind is a sphere of consciousness that transmits messages and information from the environment through the five senses, and is a recording center for impressions of all sorts. These thoughts, ideas, feelings, memories, and various emotional reactions are selectively filtered from the mind through the brain, which also functions as a storehouse for such things. Since the mind is a field of consciousness that is not limited to the individual, people are susceptible to a wide range of thoughts, feelings, and ideas. The fact that we are often telepathically aware of these impressions simultaneously, without any direct contact, speaks to this point. **Telepathy** is *communication of thoughts and ideas by means other than the known senses.*

Needless to say, our consciousness is constantly shifting across the three planes of awareness (physical, emotional, and mental) as we react to stimuli from our environment. At the same time, our sense of the world is determined by the point where our consciousness is centered. If the consciousness is focused on the emotional plane, our vision will be conditioned by our feeling nature. If our consciousness is centered on the concrete level of mind, then our orientation will be governed by thought. This explains why some people are resistant to ideas while others remain aloof from their feeling nature. The distribution of men and women across these planes of consciousness underscores the problems of communication and comprehension which are at the root of the human condition.

Our physical, emotional, and mental aspects of self, when integrated and aligned, constitute a personality. The **personality** consists of *the combined characteristics or qualities that form an individual's distinctive behavior.* One might also define a personality as *the seat of intelligent activity.* So is the question *Who are you?* answered by the fact that we have a personality? For all practical purposes we might say yes, but at the same time the personality, like the other tangible aspects of our being, is impermanent, meaning that after death it cease to exist.

For the most part, the social scientists, like those in other academic fields, take such a perspective to be axiomatic, ignoring such existential questions as *Is there a life after death?* and *Does existence precede birth?* The question revolves around another question, *What is life?* The common answer is that life is the condition that distinguishes animals and plants from inorganic matter, with the capacity for growth, reproduction, functional activity, and continual change preceding death. However, if we see death as unconsciousness and life as conscious existence, then the question takes on new meaning. A personality therefore is largely an aggregate of forms that dissolves with the cessation of consciousness and reforms when a conscious being re-emerges into another body. Assuming this is the case, the challenge to the traditional notion of life and death raises a host of inconvenient questions. From a moral standpoint, why, for instance, should millions of people be born into extreme poverty, often dying as children, while others live relatively long and happy lives in comfort? Why are some lives from the start afflicted with pain and tragedy through no fault of their own? Consequently, from the perspective of a single incarnation, human life doesn't matter much. Furthermore, how does one explain child prodigies who display complex skills and talents at a very young age without any formal training? How does one explain differentials in physique and intelligence? Why is it that people often have an innate proclivity for certain persons, places, and things? Given that the whole of nature is one repetitive cycle of birth, growth, death, and renewal, why should this be different for animals and humans? If we assume that our lives are purely accidental, then the obvious conclusion is that life itself is meaningless, apart from whatever meaning we impose upon it.

While there are a number of religious beliefs and philosophical doctrines that relate to an afterlife, the most logical assumption, though unproven, is that people live multiple lives that take place at different times and places, and in various situations and conditions. The term given to the progression of lives from one incarnation to the next is called reincarnation. So defined, **reincarnation** is *the idea that the soul, upon death of the body, comes back to earth in another body or form.* From this perspective, the notion of who we are must take account of a permanent self.

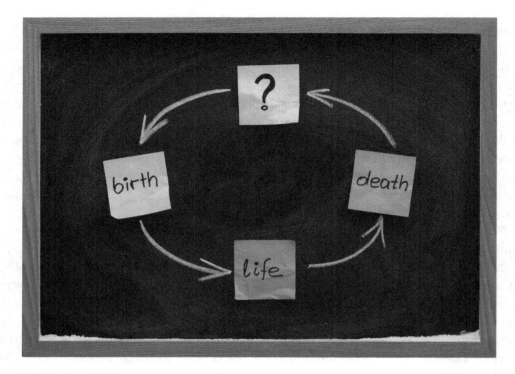

FIGURE 1.3. Reincarnation.

THE PERMANENT SELF

The idea of a permanent self may seem problematic to some people, but it has an established place in the literature of psychology, philosophy, and religion. In his book, *Gandhi's Truth*, psychologist Erik H. Erikson wrote, "Let us face it: 'deep down' nobody in his right mind can visualize his own existence without assuming he has always lived and will live hereafter ... " (25–36) Psychologist Roberto Assagioli in his book *Psychosynthesis*, makes reference to the higher self or "a permanent center of a true self" (18–19). What is being referred to here is the notion of a transpersonal self, or soul. There are many words that can be used to describe the **soul**, but suffice it to say that it is *the spiritual or immaterial part of a human being regarded as immortal.* Thus the soul may be seen as the perceiver, or the focal point of consciousness that exists whether in or out of incarnation. The word spiritual again has a wide connotation that in the lexicon of many organized religions is taken to mean something sacred or divine. Using a more scientific definition, **spirituality** may be understood as *the energies and forces which lie behind every form in nature, and which give to each of them their essential distinguishing characteristics and qualities.*

FIGURE 1.4. Spirituality.

The energy referred to in the above definition is light. What is light? Physicists refer to pockets of photons (light particles) that exist in an electromagnetic field that give rise to a whole spectrum of waves. If light is a fundamental aspect of life, it follows that the soul is a fundamental aspect of our being. References to light are frequently used as metaphors in language. We talk about someone who is wise, rational, and open-minded as being enlightened, or a person who is smart as bright. "Seeing the light" refers to a recognition of what is good or true. Thus, light is taken to mean that which elevates, enriches, and dignifies life. Since light is pervasive in all forms of life, and cannot be destroyed, it is the permanent aspect of our being through which all things are created, evolve, disintegrate, and are then reborn. Thus in the final analysis, who we are is the light of the soul.

THE IMPORTANCE OF SOUL-CENTERED SOCIOLOGY

Since all academic disciplines involve the relationship of cause and effect, the importance of the soul as the primary cause of who we are is necessary to establish a context for the study of human society. Thus the soul, which is the essence of our being, is the source of ideas. An **idea** is *any conception existing in the mind as a result of mental understanding, awareness, or activity.*[2] As ideas pass through the lower planes of the impermanent self they become distorted, since the substance of those planes is denser and tends to refract soul light. On the level of the concrete mind, ideas, generated as thoughts, are open to interpretation and may take on *a deceptive appearance or impression.* This is what is meant by the term **illusion**. On the plane of the emotions, ideas are subject to **glamour**, which is *an attractive quality that exaggerates and distorts a thought, idea, or object, giving it an appeal or special quality.* Advertisers are adept at glamorizing an object to make it more attractive and desirable. What this means is that we, in our various societies, usually do not see the world clearly and often mistake the appearance of things for what is real, or that which is soul-infused.

Let us take an example. The idea of freedom is a universal concept. It is a state of mind that relates to the notion of liberation, or that which is unrestricted. As we know, freedom has many definitions and is often used to explain or justify thoughts and actions that have little relation to its original meaning. Even those people whose intent is to limit, deny, or take away one's freedom will cloak their intentions using the idea of freedom. Thus sociology can be seen as the study of limited perceptions and how they condition social behavior.

The challenge for the student of sociology, therefore, is to ask questions and to always look for the cause behind the effect at whatever level. Sociologist Peter Berger wrote that the first wisdom of sociology is that things are not what they seem. What he meant by that statement is that those things that are interesting and important about a society are often hidden from view, and it is the job of the student to "enquire the way" in order to find a deeper level of meaning.

Supposing by analogy you were walking down a residential street with rows of houses. The houses and their settings would be obvious to the eye, although your senses might pick up different impressions from those of someone else walking the same street. Yet, the sort of interactions taking place within those homes would be unknown to you. Sociology beckons us to conceptually enter those dwellings to understand the human dynamics taking place therein. More than just the behaviors, one would be interested in the types of feelings expressed by the residents, the interchange of thoughts, and the level of consciousness that underscore such interactions. Thus what might on the surface appear normal and serene could mask a sphere of life that is volatile, unexpected, interesting, and unusual. Consequently, the question

---

2   Dictionary.com, s.v. "idea," https://www.dictionary.com/browse/idea.

Who are you? guides one along an unending path of enquiry into the world in which we live, move, and have our being. Sociology invites you to take this journey.

STUDY QUESTIONS

1. Discuss the extent to which our sense of self is a reflection of conscious awareness.
2. Why might it be said that our perceptions of the world around us are largely distortions?
3. How might sociology help one to answer the question: Who are you?

Figure Credits

CHAPTER TWO

Theoretical Perspectives

LET US START with the question, *What is sociology?* So defined, **sociology** *is the systematic and scientific study of human society.* What do we mean by a systematic and logical study? As a science, sociology studies society as a logical system that bases knowledge on direct, systematic observations. In point of fact, we are all sociologists to a degree by virtue of the fact that by living in society we need to somehow make sense of the world around us. However, our perceptions of the social world are often impressionable, incomplete, and unsystematic, not to mention distorted. Thus sociology helps us to better understand the

FIGURE 2.1. Sociology.

world we live in. Going a step further, there is the question, *What is human society?* Essentially, **society** is defined as *people who interact in a defined territory and share a culture.*

Through sociology, which focuses on the three planes (physical, emotional, and mental) of the impermanent self, we can look at the social world on two distinct levels. **Macrosociology** *is the study of large-scale,*

FIGURE 2.2. Society.

13

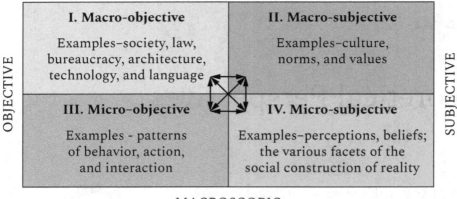

FIGURE 2.3. Macro/Micro Sociology.

long-term social processes. **Microsociology** *is a detailed study of what people do and say.* If one were to analyze crime statistics in the United States from 1900 to the present, or compare the population compositions of Brazil and Canada, they would be doing macrosociology. Conversely, an examination of conversation topics of men and women at a neighborhood gathering would comprise microsociology.

People often talk about society as something apart from themselves, as in, "Society made me do it." This individual perspective is false, since by definition we are all part of society. What this means is that rather than society being something external, the values, rules customs, and other such things that structure the social world are part of who we are in much the same way as are our thoughts, feelings, and emotional reactions. While American culture emphasizes individualism and the idea that the individual "can make a difference," it is within the reinforcing patterns of society that people think and act out the dramas (or comedies) of their lives. Popular magazines that highlight the personal lives of celebrities, for instance, would be of little interest to a sociologist. On the other hand, celebrity culture as a phenomenon in the wider society would certainly inspire a number of questions that a sociologist would find interesting.

HISTORY AND BIOGRAPHY

The sociologist C. Wright Mills noted that sociology is the intersection of history and biography. What did he mean by that statement? According to Mills, **history** is *the unfolding of events—global, national, regional—that occur during the course of one's life.* In other words, history is the context of a person's life. **Biography** refers to *the* *milestones that mark a person's life.* Suppose, for example, you were born in 2000. Your history (as part of the GEN Z generation) would comprise events and phenomena impacting your life from the time you were born such as Facebook, Instagram, and YouTube. In much the same way, your parents, who were probably born in generation X (1961–1980), would, unlike you, have grown up prior to the use of cellphones and social media, so their formative experiences would have been much different. Your biography would consist of personal events such as birthdays, graduations, and other such happenings. In the same vein, Mills defined **issues** as *matters that transcend local environments of the individual, such as a flu epidemic or a natural disaster, that affect a wide range of people, and force a change of some sort.* **Troubles**, on the other hand, are *private misfortunes,* like losing your cellphone, that affect you alone.

SEEING THE GENERAL IN THE PARTICULAR

An important aspect of the sociological perspective is seeing the general in the particular. What this means is that the lives of individuals conform to general patterns. Supposing I were to say that in a college class, seven out of ten students will marry, those who marry will have one or two children, incomes will be based on one's level of education, women (on average) will outlive men by several years, and that individuals in the class will change jobs over the course of their careers three or more times. Why can I say this? We like to think that we have free will and that our actions are random and purely of our own making. However, this is not true. Because social patterns are firmly established, we tend to conform our behavior, more or less to these patterns. Hence, our sense of free will is greatly qualified.

FIGURE 2.4. Seeing the Strange in the Familiar.

Let us pose another question: Why do people get divorced? One can think of a number of personal reasons, such as incompatibility, infidelity, financial problems, drug or alcohol abuse, and so forth. At the same time, the rate of divorce in the United States has climbed drastically since the 1960s, although it has declined somewhat in recent years. The question is why? One could point to the fact that over this period, divorce has become more socially acceptable, losing the stigma that existed three or four generations ago. By the same token, divorce is easier to obtain in most states. Also, women, thanks to changes in social norms, are more financially independent. These social factors have facilitated the rise in the number of divorces for whatever personal reasons a couple may have for going through a divorce.

Because society is structured by social patterns, sociologists are able to place people into certain categories, according to certain kinds of behavior. You can probably think of many categories that pertain to your own life such as being a student, a son or daughter, an African-American, a significant other, an athlete, musician, and so forth. Each of these categories relates to certain common characteristics. For instance students attend classes, study, take exams, and participate in various college functions. They of course have certain individual characteristics, but their patterns of behavior are usually similar.

SEEING THE STRANGE IN THE FAMILIAR

This aspect of the sociological perspective is less about searching for weird and bizarre elements in society than looking beyond the superficial and obvious.

Let us take a seemingly innocuous question like *Why do people marry*? Perhaps the most immediate answer would be because two people love each other and want to spend their lives together. This may be so, but on reflection there are many reasons why people decide to marry, which may include a desire for economic stability, peer or family pressure, sexual access, and social expectations. Probing further, we would find that a growing number of people choose not to marry, that more people today prefer to remain single, and that some of those who marry enter into same sex partnerships. The question then becomes, *What does this tell us about current social attitudes regarding marriage*? The answers may be surprising.

In the realm of politics, matters of significance often occur behind the scenes. *Why do countries go to war*? The most direct answer might be because one country is threatened by another nation-state, or it could be an expression of arrogant national pride. On the other hand, there are less obvious possibilities. If one looks at the global trade in arms sales, it is evident that this is a massive enterprise. According to a report from the Stockholm International Peace Research Institute, arms sales around the world totaled thirty-one billion dollars in 2016, the highest point in arms buildup since the end of the Cold War in 1991. Of this amount, the United States contributed

$9.9 billion in arms sales, followed by Russia with $6.4 billion. Considering that there is a correlation between the availability of weapons of mass destruction and the propensity to engage in armed conflict, one might conclude that the manufacturing and sale of weapons is a contributing factor as to why countries go to war. It might be noted that during the Vietnam War in the 1960s, the trade in arms was steadily on the increase.

GENERALIZATIONS AND STEREOTYPES

Since sociologists rely on generalizations to make sense of society, one might legitimately ask whether sociology is merely a set of stereotypes. A **generalization** is defined as *a general statement or concept obtained by inference from special cases.* A **stereotype** is *a widely-held and oversimplified image or idea of a particular type of person or thing.* There is a formula for a stereotype which is: "all (whatever group you wish to highlight) is (whatever characteristic you wish to ascribe to that group)." Since stereotypes are rigid and inflexible, they often lend themselves to bigotry and bias. Sociologists, on the other hand:

1. do not apply generalizations to all people, knowing that within any group there are many unique differences
2. make sure that generalizations square with facts so they have some legitimacy
3. use generalizations to get to the truth and willingly discard them if they prove to be false or inadequate

Generalizations are thus a tool of convenience, created to help clarify an issue and discarded when they are no longer useful. At the same time, they challenge so-called common-sense views of the world, which are often based on stereotypes, selective experiences, or unverified information.

Because all people are not the same, it is the task of the sociologist to develop categories of those who share common characteristics. For instance, there are those who on the basis of poverty, race, ethnicity, physical disability, or intellectual capacity are marginalized in society. **Marginalization** is *the treatment of a group as insignificant or peripheral.* Generalizations about marginalized groups may take into account quantitative information such as the size of the group, age, sex, and race along with other factors that are easily measured. Also included may be quantitative factors such as lifestyle and the nature of relationships. Identification of marginalized groups often leads to the ascription of certain characteristics that may or may not be true. If untrue, they can be discarded. On the other hand, making distinctions between groups can bring to light problems and issues that need to be addressed. Government policies often rely on data and theories (based on generalizations) produced by sociologists.

FIGURE 2.5. Marginalized Social Groups.

THE GLOBAL PERSPECTIVE

Whether influenced directly or indirectly, we are rapidly becoming part of a global society. While the focus of our lives is for the most part on local and personal matters, global issues are increasingly impacting us. Whether it is the products we buy, the food we eat, the information technology we use, or many other things, the chances are that these things were made or produced, in whole or in part, outside the United States. This is only the tip of the iceberg. **Globalization** is defined as *the process by which businesses or other organizations develop international influences or start operating on an international scale.*[1] Although a sovereign nation, the United States is seen increasingly as part of the world community. While nations can be divided into groups based on income levels or a standard of living, globalization has blurred some of these distinctions. According to the CIA World Factbook, the United States and most of the western post-industrialized nations have around 13 to 16% of their populations living below the poverty line. India, Mexico, and Indonesia, which have massive populations, vary considerably as to rates of poverty. Oil-rich countries such as the tiny United Arab Emirates, located next to the Persian Gulf on the Arabian Peninsula, and a much larger country, Nigeria in West Africa, have much different poverty rates. The former is around 19.5%, while the latter is 70%. Many countries in sub-Saharan Africa have poverty rates between 50% and 70%. Economic development is also a useful category in the grouping of nations, but here again, globalization is modernizing all parts of the world to a greater or lesser degree.

---

1   Oxford Living Dictionaries, s.v. "globalization," https://en.oxforddictionaries.com/definition/globalization.

FIGURE 2.6. Globalization.

If we were to reduce the earth's population of 7 billion to a village of 100, what would be its composition? The village would comprise 61 people from Asia including 19 from China and 18 from India. There would be 15 people from Africa, 10 village members would be Europeans, 9 would come from South America and the Caribbean, and the rest (5) from North America. Eighty-two villagers would be from poorer regions of the world with an average income of $5,440 a year, the equivalent of $15 of disposable income a day. The other 18 villagers would be much better off with a yearly disposable income of $32,470, or $90 a day. The native languages of the villagers would be spread out among the 6,000 languages spoken on the planet with Mandarin Chinese the most dominant, followed by English, Spanish, and Hindi or Bengali with a scattering of other languages. Clearly, most of the people in our village, and consequently around the world, would look, speak, eat, and worship differently from the average American.

THEORY AND THEORETICAL PARADIGMS

Sociologists seek to explain the world though the use of theories. A **theory** is *a statement of how and why certain facts are related*. We can think of many theories such as the theory of evolution, the theory of relativity, or the big bang theory. However, theories can be very simple and commonplace. "It usually rains on the weekend" is a theory, or "people tend to be in a better mood on Friday than Monday." In each case the definition holds since it concerns the relationship of facts into a single statement. Indeed, we use theories all the time, and are usually unaware that we are doing so.

Theories are reflections of Theoretical Paradigms which are at the heart of the sociological perspective. A **paradigm** is *a model, a typical example, or pattern of something.* A **theoretical paradigm** is *a basic image of society that guides thinking and research.*[2] The key phrase is "basic image" since one cannot study something that one can't first imagine. Theoretical paradigms provide the basis for theories, so theories are predicated on a sense of how a society works. At the same time, these paradigms are limited viewpoints since on the lower mental plane where concrete thoughts are expressed there is a diversity of perspectives. Images of society vary according to one's level of consciousness. Since a theoretical paradigm is a cognitive image, it is the product of the concrete mind. Overall, there are three fundamental theoretical paradigms in sociology.

The first is the **structural-functional** paradigm. So defined, it is *a framework for building theory that sees society as a complex system whose parts work together to promote solidarity and stability.*[3] Let us break down this definition. A framework for building theory simply means that it is a theoretical paradigm. The idea that society is a complex system whose parts work together has universal applications. Take an elaborate institution like a college. It is a system that has many parts including administration in all its many grades, faculty, support staff, college police, janitorial staff, cafeteria staff, librarians, not to mention students among others. Accordingly, if all the parts do their job then the college operates in a functional manner. If not, it is dysfunctional.

Let's look at the terms structure and function. **Social structure** refers to *any relatively stable patters of social behavior.* Take a classroom. A class consists of repetitive patterns of behavior such as lecturing, note-taking, the use of information technology, interactive class projects, and other pedagogic activities. These social structures carry on even if one or more class members are absent. The same is true for all other institutions.

Social functions refer to *the consequences of social structures for the operation of society as a whole.* Obviously, you do not take a class just to kill time. There is a plan to taking certain classes, as part of a curriculum, towards building a degree and the acquisition of knowledge in a field of study. Thus there is a purpose or function behind your course of study.

There are two kinds of functions: **manifest functions** are *recognized and intended consequences of any social pattern*, and **latent functions** are *any consequences that are largely unrecognized and unintended.*[4] Your desire to enroll at a particular college for whatever reasons is a manifest function. While at college you may develop an interest in dramatics or meet the love of your life, which is a latent function.

---

2   "Introduction to Sociology 204–2 (lecture 1)," Oregon State University, http://oregonstate.edu/instruct/soc204/plazad/lect1.htm.

3   "Introduction to Sociology," Oregon State University.

4   "Origins of Sociology," Unknown author/organization, https://1.cdn.edl.io/6mDTuRvYbxaA8Px4NFWtaGMvxD6xJlGKdbeLgtS1UDxFb6oq.pdf

The limitations of the structural-functional paradigm are that it assumes that there is 1) a clear sense of normality in a society, which is often hard to define 2) that for the most part societies are stable and orderly, which often they are not, and 3) that there is a relative degree of equality in society. In other words, everyone is on a level playing field.

The opposite of the structural-functional paradigm is the **conflict** model. This paradigm could better be labeled the *inequality* paradigm since it deals primarily with inequality in society. So defined, it is *a framework for building theory that sees society as an arena of inequality that generates conflict and change.*[5] The inequality referred to is NOT about personal relations. Having a fight with your boyfriend or being scolded by your boss has nothing to do with the conflict paradigm. It is about institutional inequality, which would include racism, sexism, or the power relations in any hierarchical structure.

So how does it work? If we look at a corporation, it is obvious that it is a pattern of hierarchy. At the top there is upper management consisting of CEOs, CFOs, CTOs, and other such persons. Next, there is middle management who are charged with carrying out the directives of upper management. Then there are the line and office workers who produce the goods and services of the corporation. The question is what are the interests of each group? For upper management, the goal is to turn a profit, to run an efficient operation, to satisfy stockholders, and to guarantee customer satisfaction. For middle management, it is to translate the vision and goals of the corporation into practical policies. For those at the bottom of the hierarchy, their interests revolve around getting better pay and benefits, laboring under good working conditions, and having more time to follow other pursuits. Clearly, the interests of those at the top are not the same as those farther down the line, thus there is an inequality of interests.

Where there is inequality, one finds conflict. Such conflict may be violent and direct, as in a race riot or mass political confrontation, or it may be subtle as in the case of the above example. When conflict occurs, there is a need for resolution that often leads to change. A race riot may result in an investigation that leads to better community policing and programs dealing with specific complaints that were at the root of the disturbance.

The conflict paradigm also challenges the idea that we live in a society of equal opportunity. To have equal opportunity, everyone must have a comparable ability to make choices. It follows that to have equality of choice everyone must have equal resources and access to power. This is obviously not true. In this sense, the conflict model is a check on the structural-functional paradigm that assumes that there is relative equality in society. A critical evaluation of the words of politicians and other framers of public opinion would show that they reflect one or the other of these paradigms.

The limitations of the conflict paradigm are 1) that it ignores how shared values and the interdependence of roles and functions which unify members of a society, 2)

---

5 "Introduction to Sociology," Oregon State University.

that it has a political bias in promoting change and therefore diminishes impartiality, and 3) that it tends to focus on people as categories rather than as individuals.

While both the structural-functional and the conflict paradigms embody macrosociology, which concerns broad patterns that shape the whole of society, the last paradigm, the interactive model, is an example of microsociology, which is a close-up focus of social interaction in specific situations.

The **interaction** paradigm is defined as *a framework for building theory that sees society as the product of everyday interactions of people.*[6] Thus it relates to the tangible world experienced through our senses. Interaction is not only about direct communication between one or more people, but it involves all facets of communication including thoughts, perceptions, emotions, and virtually everything that makes us who we are. Implied in the interaction paradigm is the notion that attitudes and behaviors are social creations that emerge through interactive patterns. Since the interactive paradigm is based on many observations of behaviors in similar situations so as to make generalizations, it has limited use in explaining broad deductive social structures that shape our society.

Seen from the plane of the soul there is no distinctive perspective, since it represents a unified consciousness that is not distinctive or separative. Whereas the lower or concrete mind divides, complicates, and separates, the soul unifies, simplifies, and integrates. Within the light of the soul all phenomena are interrelated and interconnected. Likewise, the sense of self, which we usually think of as distinctive and unique, is subsumed within a greater and more impersonal self. Ideas and ideals that stress relationship and connectedness indicate the degree to which the soul has a grip on the personality.

STUDY QUESTIONS

1. In what ways does the sociological perspective challenge the idea that we have free will?
2. Discuss the difference between a theoretical paradigm and a theory.
3. How might one study the impact of social media from a structural–functional and a conflict perspective?

Figure Credits

---

6 "Introduction to Sociology," Oregon State University.

CHAPTER THREE

Critical Thinking

WHAT IS TRUTH? There are two definitions of truth to be considered. The first is: *that which accords with fact or reality.* The second is: *a fact or belief that is accepted as true.* There are three key concepts in these definitions, namely fact, belief, and reality. A **fact** is *a piece of information used as evidence, or information used to determine the validity of a statement.* A **belief** is *the acceptance of a statement as true without necessarily any supporting evidence.* Hence facts and beliefs relate to differing sorts of truth, underscoring an awareness of reality. Facts are objective and base truth on that which can be proven. Beliefs are subjective and are based on what one inwardly feels or holds to be true. Both these terms speak to different notions of reality pertaining to one's level of consciousness. If the consciousness is centered at the level of the emotions, one is more apt to experience reality personally as a matter of belief. On the other hand, for someone who is polarized on the concrete mental plane, their sense of reality will more likely be predicated on facts and evidence. Reality at the soul level defies definition as it is an instantaneous recognition that all phenomena is part of one stupendous whole. Thus truth, as a reflection of one's comprehension of reality, can be understood as relative or absolute.

The importance of belaboring the question of truth is highlighted by the fact that the nature of reality has recently been called into question. The reverence for information based on facts has become distorted by so-called "alternative facts," which are untrue or exaggerated statements masquerading as truths. Alternative facts are usually couched in **opinions** that are *personal statements, often biased or prejudiced that are not necessarily supported by facts.* Such distortions are harmful to the health of any society, which is functional only when there is clear and accurate thinking. It might be said that one of the fundamental problems in society is the inability to delineate truth from fiction, or even to think at all. The impact of false facts on collective thinking is hard to gauge but there is some evidence. According to a poll conducted by the Public Religion Research Institution, a large percentage of Americans hold the unlikely belief that they or a member of their family will be a victim of terrorism.

According to the Washington Post–Kaiser Foundation poll, there is a growing discontent between Americans worried about global warming and federal government officials within the Trump administration who have aggressively scaled back environmental regulations. Based on a Gallup poll, many people believe that politicians are corrupt, and an overwhelming number of Americans have lost confidence in the nation's institutions. These are sobering statistics based in part upon misinformation often predicated on bogus facts. Not surprisingly, less than 60% of eligible voters cast their ballots in presidential elections. In local elections, there is more like a 20% turnout.

Furthermore, advances in information technologies and the popularity of reality TV shows have created virtual realities that cause confusion and distortions. Programs that purport to show celebrities' everyday lives as turbulent, involving divorces, extra-marital affairs, and multiple sex partners, impact how the viewing public sees normative human relations. Moreover, a survey of consumers in the United States showed that 65% believe that virtual reality will change the way people shop. In order to discern the real from the unreal, critical thinking is essential.

COMMON SENSE VS. THE SCIENTIFIC METHOD

The value of the scientific approach used by sociologists in dealing with commonly held opinions is that it provides a solid basis for determining their validity. For

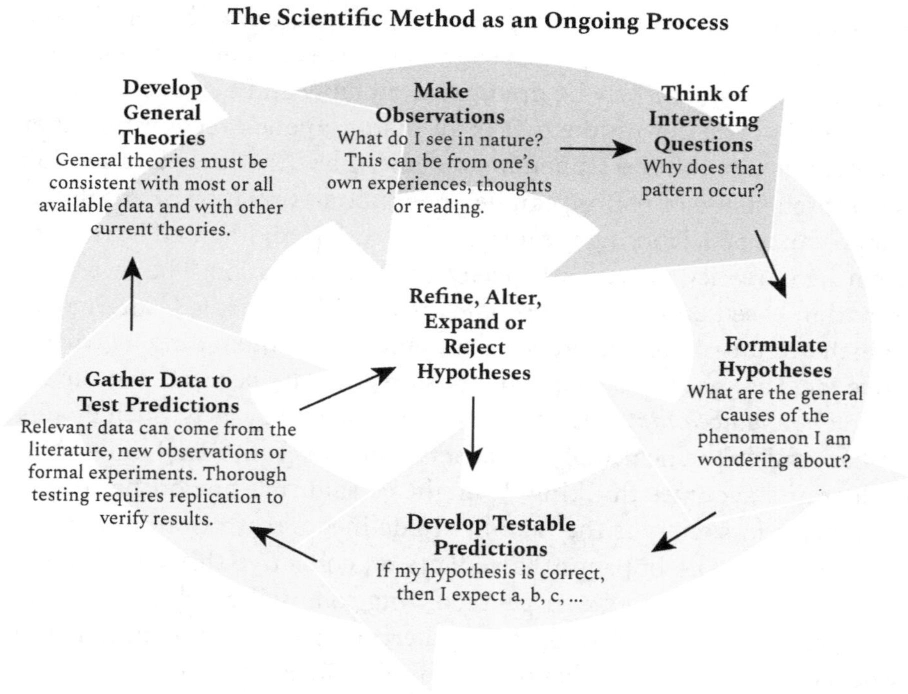

The Scientific Method as an Ongoing Process

Develop General Theories
General theories must be consistent with most or all available data and with other current theories.

Make Observations
What do I see in nature? This can be from one's own experiences, thoughts or reading.

Think of Interesting Questions
Why does that pattern occur?

Formulate Hypotheses
What are the general causes of the phenomenon I am wondering about?

Refine, Alter, Expand or Reject Hypotheses

Gather Data to Test Predictions
Relevant data can come from the literature, new observations or formal experiments. Thorough testing requires replication to verify results.

Develop Testable Predictions
If my hypothesis is correct, then I expect a, b, c, ...

FIGURE 3.1. Scientific Approach.

instance, it is widely believed that poor people are more likely to break the law than those who are affluent. However, this is not true. Research has shown that white-collar crimes (offenses committed by people of means) are far more plentiful. It is just that they are underreported and get far less attention in the media. Another myth is that poor people are lazy and do not want to work. Here again, there is solid evidence to the contrary. Poor people often work at low-paying jobs which provide insufficient income to meet their expenses. As regards public assistance, wealthy corporations and individuals are far greater recipients of government handouts than are those who qualify for welfare. Thus by examining the data, a picture of society emerges that is different from the one that is perpetuated by popular myths.

KNOWING

To know something is to establish certainty based on empirical evidence and logical thought. The question is, how do we think we know what we know? The most common and reliable way of knowing is through experience. We experience the world in different ways all the time. When a child touches a hot stove and burns a finger, he or she quickly learns to be more careful around such appliances. While experience enables us to better function in society, at the same time it often does not provide an accurate picture of the social world. If a person has a bad interaction with someone of a different race or ethnic group, for example, and if that experience creates a negative stereotype about that race or group, then that interaction will have conveyed a false message.

Statements from other people, particularly those in authority (like parents and teachers) also add to our reservoir of knowledge, even though they may, in the course of time, be proven wrong. Likewise, public opinion feeds us information that we often accept, especially when there is no contrary evidence. This can be dangerous since unverified information, often presented as propaganda or a sales pitch for something or other, is one-sided even if it conveys a grain of truth. Overall, what we claim to know is information internalized from a number of sources that may or may not be true.

In order to counteract false knowledge, one needs to cultivate principles of critical thinking. Such principles are as follows:

- Be skeptical.
- Examine the definitions of terms and concepts.
- Examine the assumptions or premises of stated comments or arguments.
- Be cautious about drawing conclusions from the evidence that is presented.
- Consider other possible explanations.
- Do not simplify or over-generalize.
- Apply critical thinking to all aspects of life.

These principles can be summed up in a series of self-reflective questions:

1. What am I being asked to accept or believe?
2. What evidence is there to support an assertion or argument?
3. Are there alternative ways of interpreting the evidence?
4. What additional evidence is needed to evaluate alternatives?
5. Based on the evidence, what conclusions are the most reasonable?

Clear thinking is rooted in a spirit of curiosity and a desire to go beyond surface explanations. Again, we cannot forget the importance of definitions. Often people who engage in a debate or argument have little idea what they are talking about because they have not taken the time to define their terms. Two people of different political persuasions, for instance, may frequently use words like freedom, choice, and opportunity, but what do they mean by those terms? The chances are they differ as to the meaning of the concepts in question even though the terminology is the same. Unless one defines what they mean by the words they use, the argument gets lost.

It is also essential to examine the assumptions behind a given argument. What is meant by the phrase "a right to life"? For someone who is opposed to abortion, the phrase would be interpreted as protection for a fetus or unborn child. For someone supportive of a woman's right to choose whether to have an abortion or not, a right to life could mean giving a child sufficient resources to enjoy a comfortable and productive existence.

There are numerous logical fallacies that one needs to be on guard against such as: **false analogy**, which is assuming that because certain things are true of one factor they are automatically true of another factor; **misuse of terms**, for instance referring to low paid workers as slaves when in fact a slave is a person who is owned by someone else; **appeals to authority**, or the citing of expert opinion without any supportive evidence;

thou shalt not commit logical fallacies

- strawman
- false cause
- appeal to emotion
- the fallacy fallacy
- slippery slope
- ad hominem
- tu quoque
- personal incredulity
- special pleading
- loaded question
- the gambler's fallacy
- bandwagon
- appeal to authority
- composition/ division
- no true scotsman
- genetic
- black-or-white
- begging the question
- appeal to nature
- anecdotal

FIGURE 3.2. Logical Fallacies.

and **improper inference**, which is an assumption derived from a statement that is not accurate.

TYPES OF CAUSES

Logical thought as an element of critical thinking is concerned with those factors that cause something to happen, and the impact or effect it may have on a person or thing. There are two kinds of causes. The first is **efficient causes,** which is *the relation of one observable fact to another.* We deal with efficient causes all the time. Suppose your computer is malfunctioning. While you may be aware of the problem (or effect), what you are really interested in is the cause. The problem might be a software issue, defective hardware, or some other matter. By eliminating one possible cause after another, you hopefully will find the real cause of the problem. Similarly, reverse engineering is taking a finished product and retracing the steps that were followed to make it in the first place. Efficient causes, moreover, pertain to procedural activities. Whether you are baking a cake or putting together an appliance, there is a step-by-step process whereby one thing leads to another until the task or product is completed.

FIGURE 3.3. Cause and Effect.

Apart from efficient causes, there are **final causes** defined as *factors that cannot be readily comprehended or understood.* Does God exist? This is a question that is often debated but cannot be proven logically since it deals with a phenomenon that is beyond the comprehension of the concrete mind. On the other hand, if we ask the question "Does God exist as a distinctive and separate being?" then there is a basis of proof. Although this is a more advanced level of reasoning than you are expected to know, the methodology may prove to be instructive.

Definitions

1. God: superhuman being, worshipped deity; the Supreme Being.
2. exist: having being; emerge, appear, proceed, be visible or manifest
3. being: the fact of existing or existence as opposed to non-existence
4. superhuman: above and beyond what is human; having a higher nature or greater powers than man[1]
5. separate: kept apart by an intervening barrier or space; to set apart, disconnect, disassociate

Proof

1. If God is that which is being, then that which is without being is not God.
2. If being consists of life, conscious existence, and form, then that which does not have life, consciousness, and form is not God.
3. If God is a superhuman being, its primary essence is still being.
4. If a human is being, then its primary essence is still being.
5. If all other forms of existence are being, then their primary essence is still being.
6. That which is being cannot be non-being.
7. That which has life, conscious existence and form (being) cannot be dissociated or separated from itself.
8. That which is dissociated or separate from itself is not being.
9. If God is being, it cannot be disassociated or separate from itself.
10. If a human is being, it cannot be disassociated or separate from itself.
11. If other forms of existence are being, they cannot be disassociated or separate from themselves.
12. If God as being cannot be disassociated or separate from itself, it cannot be separate or disassociated from other such beings.

Conclusion
Therefore, God cannot exist as a distinctive and separate being.

---

1 *American Heritage® Dictionary of the English Language*, 5th ed., s.v. "superhuman," https://www.thefreedictionary.com/Super-human.

SYLLOGISMS

A **syllogism** *is a form of reasoning in which a conclusion is drawn (whether validly or not) from two given or assumed propositions (premises), each of which shares a term with the conclusion, and shares a common or middle term not present in the conclusion.*[2] Essentially, a syllogism is a logical construct that conforms to a simple formula: If A=B, and B=C, then: A=C. Syllogisms include a major premise, a minor premise, and a conclusion. Let's look at an example.

1. Sociology is the science of society (major premise).
2. Science is a logical system that bases knowledge on direct systematic observation (minor premise).
3. Therefore: sociology is a logical system that bases knowledge on direct systematic observation (conclusion).

As an element of language, a syllogism consists of a thesis and a reason in a single sentence. Using the example "music has a strong moral impact on young people," *music* is the subject, which is what the statement is about, *young people* is the object which relates to the meaning of the statement, and the predicate to be proven is *strong moral impact.* The completed syllogism would be:

1. Music conveys a strong moral impact.
2. Young people are influenced by music.
3. Therefore, music has a strong moral impact on young people.

It is important to note that the premise upon which a syllogism is based may or may not be true. While music may or may not have a moral impact on young people, having accepted the premise as true, the syllogism carries it to a logical conclusion.

Critical thinking is not easy and involves a constant evaluation of what we think, say, and interpret from a variety of outside sources. In essence, the ability to think critically is about looking for the cause(s) behind the effect. This is an ongoing process since whatever the effect there is always a precipitating cause, whether it is a material (impermanent) phenomenon or something abstract and metaphysical. Critical thinking is the only means by which one can discern the cause beyond the effect, and ultimately truth from falsehood. The old adage "Know the truth and the truth will make you free" is a thought well worth pondering.

---

2   Oxford Living Dictionaries, s.v. "syllogism," https://en.oxforddictionaries.com/definition/syllogism.

STUDY QUESTIONS

1. Using the tools of reason and logic, how might one analyze whether the statement, "Americans have a better quality of life than other nations" is true or false?

2. Devise a syllogism from the phrase "Facebook compromises one's right to privacy."

3. Discuss the distinction between efficient and final causes, and give an example of each.

Figure Credits

CHAPTER FOUR

Methods of Research

HAVING SURVEYED THE sociological perspective and the challenges of critical thinking, we will now consider how sociologists go about doing research. Since we have established that sociology is a scientific approach to the study of society, it follows that there must be a systematic method of gathering information so as to provide evidence in support of theories and generalizations. One of the pioneers of sociology, Auguste Comte, coined the term **positivism** as *a way of understanding the world through science.* Bear in mind that as a scientific approach, sociology is limited to explanations of the phenomenal world. Even though the complexities of human existence go beyond concrete scientific analysis, the scientific method, as a way making sense of our surroundings, is indispensable.

BASIC ELEMENTS

The starting point for a scientific investigation is to define key terms. The first is **concept,** which is *a mental construct that represents some part of the world in a simplified form.*[1] Most sentences contain one or more concepts, which are nouns describing a person, place, or thing. The word book, for instance, is a concept because it represents all books. Clearly, there are innumerable other examples. Sociologists use concepts when referring to social groups.

A **variable** is *a concept that changes from case to case.* The concept class (as in social class) might refer to people within a certain income range in one instance, and to those falling within particular occupational groupings in another instance. In order for a variable to be useful, it must be measured. This is called **operationalizing a variable**. Supposing for instance we were planning to study the proportion of middle-class people in a given city. Middle

---

1   "Sociology 204-02 Lecture 2," Oregon State University, http://oregonstate.edu/instruct/soc204/plazad/lect2.htm.

class is a concept, but what does it mean? It could refer to wealth, income social status, level of education, ancestry, or some other factor. By designating this concept in terms of income, it takes the form of a variable. The question is then, what range of income constitutes middle class? If we say, for the sake of argument, that a middle class income falls within the range of $30,000 and $150,000 then we will have operationalized the variable.

In order to make this variable useful, it must be reliable. **Reliability** refers to *consistency in measurement*. This means that if other researchers performed the same experiment, there would need to be a similarity of results. At the same time, a piece of research needs to have **validity**, which is *precisely measuring what one intends to measure*. Suppose for instance we were interested in studying how many people in a given community are religious. As a research plan, we decide to count the number of individuals who go to church each Sunday and calculate those findings in relation to the total population. The flaw in this research is that one is not measuring the religiosity of a community since some people who go to church may not be religious, and those who stay away may have strong religious convictions. All we have done in this hypothetical study is to determine the percentage of people who go to church each Sunday. Therefore, the research plan is not valid.

CAUSE-AND-EFFECT VARIABLES

Once we have settled upon a valid topic to be studied, and have operationalized the variables, the next step is to determine cause and effect. *The variable that causes change* is called the **independent variable**, and *the variable that is changed* is the **dependent variable**. Usually the dependent variable is already known since it is the effect of something that has happened. A person lying dead on a street would be the dependent variable. How this came about remains a mystery and could be the result of a number of causes or independent variables. Did the man collapse from heat exhaustion or a heart attack? Was the cause a drug overdose? Was he hit by a vehicle? Was he shot or attacked by another person? These are unknowns that would need to be determined. A detective investigating this matter would gather information from the victim's body and/or from possible by-standers so as to reconstruct what happened. In the process, the detective would eliminate those independent variables that did not fit the evidence until the relevant cause was isolated. Often sociological research is a repetitive process of isolating particular independent variables through a controlled experiment.

The method of determining which independent variables are effective causes is through establishing correlations. A **correlation** is *a relationship between two or more variables*. Suppose that a team of researchers was studying the rise of juvenile delinquency in a given neighborhood. They initially found a link between the fact that the population of the region consisted largely of young people and the propencity

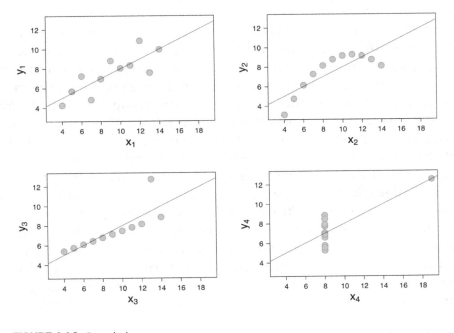

FIGURE 4.1A. Correlation.

to engage in delinquent behavior. Next, they found that there was a large number of illicit drugs sold in that neighborhood, which could also correlate with increased crime. The team then jumped to the conclusion that because the earlier correlation had been established, there was also a connection between the existence of a large population of young people and drug dealing. This would be a **spurious correlation**

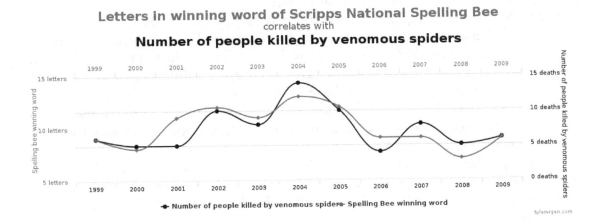

FIGURE 4.1B. Spurious Correlation.

which is *a false relationship between two or more variables*. Even though the correlations between a rise in juvenile delinquency and the initial two variables had been established, there was little evidence to support any connection between drug availability and a young population. In fact, drug dealing often involves an older cohort group.

Sorting out legitimate correlations from spurious correlations requires the designation of control and experimental groups. A **control group** is *a group of subjects in a research experiment that is not subject to the independent variable*. An **experimental group** is *a group of subjects that is exposed to the independent variable*. Suppose that a group of researchers wished to test whether a particular drug would cure a certain illness. The researchers would first make sure that the experimental group who had the illness contained the same demographics pertaining to race/ethnicity, gender, and other relevant factors as the control group. They would then give the experimental group the drug and dispense a placebo to the control group. Next, they would test to see if the health of the experimental group showed a significant improvement over the control group, all other variables being equal. Many experiments, particularly those involving pharmaceuticals, must be replicated by other researchers using the same procedures so as to avoid any bias or distortion in the original experiment.

Research Orientations

The approaches to gathering research information correspond to the three sociological paradigms. The first, based on the structural–functional model, is the **scientific or objective** approach, which is *a personal position of neutrality when doing research*. It is a quantitative method used most often in collecting and computing vast amounts of data. A survey of voter preferences across the country would utilize this methodology. Objective research purports to be value-free insofar as the researcher allows the information gathered to speak for itself thus eliminating, as far as possible, personal bias.

The **interpretive approach**, which relates to the interactive paradigm, is subjective, or *a study of society that focusses on the meanings people place on their observations*, and is thus based on a qualitative approach to data gathering. **Qualitative** refers to *an exploration of the reasons, thoughts, and opinions one has of a particular topic*. In this instance, the researcher might be involved with the object of his or her study. For example, if a sociologist was interested in studying political involvement by an environmental organization, he or she might become a member, or attend their meetings so as to participate in the activities of that group. The object of the researcher would be to interpret what was said and done and thus draw conclusions based on such observations.

Conflict theorists often use the **critical approach** as a *means of bringing about a change in the way groups and institutions function*. Such an approach might involve, for instance, collecting data on instances of police harassment of black citizens so as to initiate changes in policing policies. Activists who pursue this line of research are usually interested in power relationships between different social groups.

Each of these orientations has its limitations. Because the scientific approach relies on human predictability, it often does not take into account exceptions that do not fit the rule. Social patterns vary according to situations so the collection of data on a wide scale might contain some distortions. Also, while the scientific approach purports to be neutral, the question arises as to whether it can ever be totally value-free given that everyone looks at the social world through the limitations of their own perspectives. While the interactive approach has the advantage of providing access to more in-depth and subtle information than that obtained through objective research, it relies on the perceptions of the researcher. There is what is called a **Hawthorne effect,** which is *a change in a subject's behavior caused by the awareness of being studied.*[2] Also, such in-depth investigations are limited to small groups that can be observed, so the information gained will be from far fewer samples than can be obtained through objective research. By the same token, observations are tied to specific times and places, which limits the scope for broader interpretations. The critical approach can be challenged for being inherently biased towards a particular social group. Accordingly, inconvenient facts that do not support the intended conclusions of the research are sometimes ignored.

Methods of Research

There are four basic research methods used by sociologists to gather data. The scientific approach relies heavily on **questionnaires** or *a set of printed or written questions with a choice of answers, devised for the purposes of a survey or statistical study.*[3] Questionnaires are used to provide a sizeable sample from a large population group. Such questionnaires usually call for clear-cut yes/no or short answer responses that allow for statistical analysis. Its shortcoming is that the reasons for why or how, which require more elaborate explanations, are difficult to obtain.

This problem can be addressed through interviews utilizing a qualitative methodology. An **interview** is simply *a conversation where questions are asked and answers are given.* The researcher is then able to ask follow-up questions and listen to the responses of subjects so as to abstract key concepts or phrases that may fit into a pattern compiled through other interviews. In some cases, an initial response by a subject may be contradicted by further questions, which may put the topic in a different light. Again, the reliability of this research method relies on the un-biased perspective of the researcher.

Sociologists commonly set up **experiments** *which are scientific processes to test hypotheses or demonstrate known facts.* Experiments are used to study how people will react in various situations. Usually this involves introducing a variable into the

---

2   "Sociology Lecture 2," Oregon State University.

3   Oxford Living Dictionaries, s.v. "questionnaire," https://en.oxforddictionaries.com/definition/questionnaire.

experiment. In a highly publicized experiment, Philip Zimbardo created a prison in the basement of the Stanford psychology department to test whether the prison experience was the cause of violent behavior. He recruited a group of young men and divided them randomly into guards and prisoners. The actors played out their roles so realistically that the experiment had to be aborted when a number of the prisoners developed severe emotional distress. What the experiment showed was that prison violence was rooted in the social interactions of prison life. Experiments are legion and may be as simple as violating a social rule to test people's adherence to conformity.

FIGURE 4.2. Gathering Data.

Another research methodology is **participant observation**, which is *a research method used to systematically observe people engaged in normal activities.*[4] Supposing a researcher was interested in how males and females interact in a social situation. He or she might take up a position in a bar or social club, frequented by members of both sexes, and watch the various interactions among them based on a pre-conceived hypothesis or set of research questions. Such an observation, of course, would have to be replicated numerous times in similar situations to be able to deduce a consistent pattern of behavior.

A final research method is **secondary analysis,** which is *the reanalysis of either qualitative or quantitative data already collected in a previous study* by a different researcher

---

4 "Sociology Lecture 2," Oregon State University.

normally wishing to provide a basis for further study or search for a new research question.[5] Much research already exists in published form that allows a sociologist to review what has already been done so as to formulate new questions or test existing ones. If a sociologist was interested in investigating sexual harassment in the armed forces, for instance, he or she would find that the military had already compiled numerous studies on the subject that would frame or provide a solid basis for further research.

Steps in Sociological Research

Having identified the various approaches and methodologies for doing research, it is time to put it all together. One must first have a **topic** in mind. Let's suppose that we are interested in studying the relationship between participation in college sports and academic performance. Once we have selected a topic, our next step is to **research the subject**. Have there been other similar studies? What questions are raised in sports and academic journals that are pertinent to the topic?

Next comes the **hypothesis**, which is defined as *a supposition or proposed explanation made on the basis of limited evidence as a starting point for further investigation.*[6] Put simply, a hypothesis is an educated guess about the relationship between variables. The hypothesis is the linchpin for any research since it puts forth the question or problem to be studied. In the course of doing background research, we might decide to hypothesize: "Students who engage in college sports spend less time studying for their courses than do students who are not college athletes." Naturally, we need to operationalize this hypothesis so it can be measured. We will take less study time to mean one to five hours a week as opposed to those who study in excess of ten hours.

Our next step is to decide on a **research plan**. Vital to this or any research would be to determine the size of the sample population and to ensure that the control group (non-student athletes) contain the same demographics as the experimental group (student athletes). The study should be comprehensive enough to account for distortions in the data. For the sake of this study, since we will be focusing on students at a particular institution, the interview method would seem appropriate so as to find out about a person's study habits and the length of time they spent preparing for their courses. The interview process could be based on set questions and/or open-ended questions to allow the person interviewed to elaborate further on any point.

---

5   Geoff Payne and Judy Payne, "Secondary Analysis," In *Key Concepts in Social Research* (SAGE Publications, 2004), Retrieved from http://methods.sagepub.com/book/key-concepts-in-social-research/n45.xml.

6   Oxford Living Dictionaries, s.v. "hypothesis," https://en.oxforddictionaries.com/definition/hypothesis.

In all research, attention must be given to ethical concerns, such as the privacy of the subjects involved.

Once our research plan is in place, the next step is to **gather the data** by doing an extensive series of interviews with the identified subjects. This often takes a considerable amount of time, and follow-up interviews are sometimes necessary. Once the interviews are complete, then we need to **analyze the data** by looking through the responses to determine the amount of study time for each cohort group. From this analysis, certain **conclusions** may be drawn that relate back to the hypothesis. The conclusions may support or refute the hypothesis. On the other hand, they may prove to be inconclusive, in which case further data may be required or the hypothesis itself may need to be re-worked. Often the results of a study raise questions for further research.

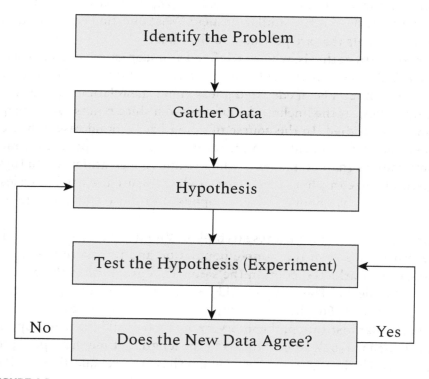

FIGURE 4.3. Scientific Research step-by-step.

As you can see, sociological research is a tenacious step-by-step process that requires considerable patience and attention to detail.

STUDY QUESTIONS

1. If you were part of a research team studying the extent of racism at your college, what sort of hypothesis might you propose and what would be the most appropriate research tools to study this problem?

2. Compare and contrast objective, subjective, and critical approaches to research. What are the strengths and weaknesses of each method?

3. If one wished to study student–teacher relations in a classroom, what would be the most effective method of research to use, and why?

Figure Credits

Fundamental Ideas of the Social World

HUMAN EXISTENCE IS based upon ideas that lend themselves to a variety of social patterns. Chapters Five to Eight seek to explore these basic ideas. The first is culture, which is a qualitative summation of human experience, inclusive of ideas, rules, values, beliefs, and tangible objects. Culture is at once universal and differentiated according to civilizations and societies. A civilization deals with qualitative characteristics of human development, whereas a society relates to interactions between peoples within a particular territory who enjoy a common culture. Socialization is the process of cultural learning over the course of the life cycle. More particularly, it pertains to the complex question of human nature, relating back to the human constitution as discussed in the first chapter. The sociological construction of reality deals with the issue of defining reality in the course of everyday life. Central to a sense of reality is one's focus of consciousness that gives to a person his or her framework for understanding themselves and the world around them.

CHAPTER FIVE

Culture

CULTURE IS NOT an easy term to define, and it can be characterized in different ways. The word sometimes refers to the arts, the manifestations of human intellectual achievement, or an integrated pattern of human knowledge. At the same time, culture implies a relationship between the realm of meaning and the outer world of human endeavor. Meaning can be interpreted differently depending upon one's conscious perception. From the angle of the soul, meaning is generated in terms of synthetic patterns, conveyed symbolically through ideas. The concrete mind interprets these ideas as ideals (or reactions to ideas), which are registered in the brain as patterns of thought that underscore the arts, ideologies, and other forms of intellectual endeavor. Sensitivity to these ideals are then registered as feelings Thus culture is experienced in consciousness subjectively as well as objectively.

THE CULTURAL PERSPECTIVE

The broad characterizations of culture fit well with its sociological definition. **Culture** defined is *the totality of human experience.* Further delineated, culture can be material, meaning tangible objects, or that which is non-material—ideas, for instance. The importance of culture, first of all, is that it enables people to solve fundamental problems that facilitate human survival and social interaction. Take for example childbirth. There is much essential knowledge related to pregnancy and care for infants that is passed down through the generations, which is essential for propagating the species. At the same time, culture is relative. It is obvious that people in different nations and continents share distinctive cultures, or variations of an over-riding culture. Historically, cultures also change over time. Your grandparents will tell you that the values, way of life, and technology enjoyed by their generation were significantly different from those which you experience today. Even within a single generation, culture is constantly changing, often in very subtle ways.

The fact that cultures evolve over eons of time speaks to how emerging ideas become translated into social products. An idea that leads to the invention of a new machine will have a ripple effect throughout the society forcing numerous other changes. In other words, change in one instance stimulates many other changes.

One measure of the power of culture is **culture shock**, which is *a personal disorientation when experiencing an unfamiliar way of life.*[1] Have you ever travelled to another part of the world where people speak a different language, eat strange foods, and/or organize their society in ways that are unfamiliar to you? If so, you probably felt at a loss for a while until the social rules and patterns of that society became more familiar to you. What this shows is that your own culture is so familiar that you take it for granted without thinking about it. When confronted with an alien society, one quickly becomes aware of the diversity and pervasiveness of culture.

COMPONENTS OF CULTURE

Looking at culture sociologically, we see that it consists of numerous components, which are essentially ideals derived from ideas. Generally speaking, culture is fundamentally **symbols** which are *representations of some phenomena that carry a particular meaning.* In fact, all human behavior and civilizations emerge from an understanding and use of symbols. Indeed, it is the ability to interpret the world around us symbolically through our senses that makes us human and unique from other species. Symbols, as stated above, are conveyed through ideas on the higher planes of consciousness, and by means of ideals on the more concrete levels. Of course, the meaning we derive from symbols is dependent on our level of consciousness, which is why people often have contrasting or conflicting perceptions of the same thing.

Another component of culture is language. **Language** is *a set of symbols arranged in a certain pattern that conveys meaning to those sharing a common culture.* Language is conveyed orally by word of mouth, emblematically through the written word, and visually through pictures and images. Other symbolic representations, such as mathematics, are forms of language. Two sociologists, Edward Sapir and Benjamin Whorf developed what is known as the **Sapir-Whorf thesis** which states that *people perceive the world through the cultural lens of language.*[2] It is hard to think of anything without using language, unless one is in deep meditation, but otherwise we engage the world, both internally and externally, through a constant stream of symbols. Language is essential for **cultural transmission**, which is *the process of transmitting culture from*

---

1 "A different kind of culture shock," Cross Cultural Solutions, https://www.crossculturalsolutions.org/blog/different-kind-culture-shock.

2 "Culture," Quia, https://www.quia.com/jg/535648list.html.

one generation to another. Almost from the moment of birth, we receive information of all sorts that reveal different facets of our culture.

Values and beliefs constitute the third component of culture. **Values** are *culturally defined standards or ideals.* In other words, values are what we consider to be desirable or undesirable, good or bad. They are the basis for making assessments and judgments. If we consider one item to be of better quality than another item, we are applying a value to it. In much the same way we employ values in judging someone's behavior, perceptions, or taste. There are collective values as well as personal values. Compassion, cooperation, neighborliness, and justice are human values that are widely accepted by people around the world. Personal freedom, upward mobility, and equal opportunity are generally accepted as American values. **Beliefs** are *statements predicated on ideals considered to be true.* Many people who believe in God try to live their lives according to a set of ethical principles, spiritual ideals, or divine pronouncements in books of sacred scriptures. Whether God actually exists is not the issue. If people believe in God, then for them it is true.

Norms are another aspect of culture. Defined, **norms** are *social rules and expectations.* The fact that norms are constantly changing and evolving suggests that the ideas from which they are derived are also in a state of flux. Norms are so pervasive that we are hardly aware that they exist at all, yet our lives are structured by them. There are **proscriptive norms**, which are *things we should not do,* and **prescriptive norms** that *pertain to things we should do.* Laws, and rules of various kinds that seek to enforce behavior are examples of the former, whereas acts of charity or civility characterize the latter. Many norms *have a moral significance,* such as not harming others, respecting one's personal property, and being kind to animals. These are called **mores.** Many more norms, called **folkways**, *govern routine social situations.* The side of the dinner plate where one puts the fork, the attire a groom wears at a morning wedding (as opposed to an evening wedding), the proper format for addressing a public official, etc., are all governed by social rules even if we do not know (or care) what they are. Books on etiquette are full of folkways. **Social control** is *how a society enforces norms.* This is done in various ways. The apparatus of law enforcement, including the police, courts, and prisons is the means of securing conformity to laws and statutes. Institutions also have ways of ensuring compliance with rules. However, there are many informal ways we enforce a measure of social control in our daily lives. Since norms involve expectations, we often dole out rewards and punishments based on whether people live up to the standards (values) or patterns of behavior that we expect from others. Our expectations of how people should act are constant factors in all our interactions.

The final component of culture is material culture and technology. These two concepts are not the same. **Material culture** consists simply of *artifacts or any tangible material object,* which are numberless in their variety. Artifacts are the product of technology. **Technology** refers to *the knowledge (ideas) used to create artifacts.* Your cell

FIGURE 5.1A. Old Computer.

FIGURE 5.1B. New Computer.

phone did not just appear out of nowhere, but was the product of complex thought, analysis, knowledge, and experimentation. Technology compounds itself and is often derived from previously developed ideas. Technology as knowledge is a process of making connections and one does not often know the direction in which a line of development may lead.

CULTURAL GROUPS

Since making sense of society generally involves delineating groups with common characteristics, understanding culture requires making similar distinctions. Various forms of artistic expression fall into the categories of **high culture** and **popular culture.** High culture refers to *those artistic forms and social patterns that endure over time.* The works of Shakespeare, the music of Mozart or Beethoven, or the paintings of Rembrandt would be obvious examples. Popular culture *relates to those forms and patterns that are widespread and fashionable at any particular time but often fade away.* The varieties of popular culture are pervasive and may affect every corner of society. Likewise, some cultural aspects endure the test of time and may eventually come to be characterized as high culture.

FIGURE 5.2. High Culture.

The culture of any society contains numerous smaller groups known as **subcultures**, which are *cultural patters that distinguish a segment of the society's population in some particular way.* We are all included in a number of subcultures. Students are a subculture, as are girlfriends/boyfriends, sisters/brothers, sons/daughters, athletes, musicians, nerds, beach bums, Hispanics, Baptists, birders, bikers, and writers among many others. While the lives of people are generally normative, being part of various subcultures gives one certain distinct identities, even though they may involve no commitment or active participation. Some subcultures are not normative. They may include drug users, terrorists, gangsta rap musicians and followers, or even militant

FIGURE 5.3. Counterculture.

vegetarians. These groups may be termed **countercultures**, which are *subcultures that are in some way at odds with normal social structures.*

CULTURAL IDENTITIES

The rapid shift to a global society has brought changes in the composition and structure of populations all over the world. The face of society in the United States is much different from what it was two or three generations ago. Previously, it could be said that the country was largely assimilated predominately with Caucasian people of European descent, who were products of the Judeo-Christian tradition. Today more and more people are arriving from other parts of the world who profess different languages, religions, and other cultural traits.

Consequently, this has led to a shift in the way Americans view themselves and the rest of the world. **Ethnocentrism**, characteristic of a highly assimilated society with a distinctive majority population, is defined as *superiority of the dominant culture over all other cultures.* The corollary to ethnocentrism is the tendency to judge other cultures by the standards of one's own culture. This "us-versus-them" perspective creates a bubble of glamour and illusion that prevents those within a society from seeing people in other cultures clearly. The consequences of this attitude are reflected in the ways that alien cultures see us. For instance, massive polling data has shown that many people in the Muslim world sense that their religion is not respected in the United States, which leads to widespread feelings of humiliation, and a sense of being threatened and controlled by others. The result of this often leads to anger and a tendency towards political radicalization. On the other hand, one could argue that homogeneous societies are more stable than those consisting of diverse cultural groups.

The opposite of ethnocentrism is **multiculturalism**, defined as *the equality of all cultural traditions.* Multiculturalism, or pluralism (the diversity of population composition) sees society as a patchwork quilt of diverse cultures, each adding some trait to the existing culture. An important expression of multiculturalism is **cultural relativism**, which is a perspective by which *one judges a culture by its own standards.* This is clearly not the line of least resistance for many people who are more comfortable seeing the world through the lens of their own culture. Cultural practices in other parts of the world are often radically different from our own. Across large parts of Asia and Africa men are allowed to have more than one wife, and women in Saudi Arabia and certain other Middle Eastern countries are required to either fully cover themselves or wear some form of head or body covering like a burka, a chador, or a hijab. In other places, like Afghanistan, girls are expected to marry in their teens. While these customs may seem strange or repulsive when viewed through the norms and values of our own society, the question, from a culturally relative perspective, is to what extent do they benefit those societies that institutionalize such practices? Also, how do people in those societies view those customs that are different from our own? These questions probe deeper into the meaning and function of culture in diverse societies.

Cultures change at different rates. **Cultural integration** refers to *the close relationship among various elements of a cultural system.* Just think of how the invention of the Internet has profoundly altered the ways in which people communicate and interact with one another through e-mail, social media, and the dissemination of large amounts of data. For many, it would be hard to imagine life without such information systems. **Cultural lag** is a term used to describe *how some cultural elements change more quickly than others.* Fads and fashions often emerge within a certain subculture and then gradually spread into the wider society. The use of illicit drugs, for instance, started within the counter-cultural groups in the late 1960s and gradually spread into the mainstream a decade later. The same could be said about the so-called sexual revolution.

THEORETICAL PERSPECTIVES OF CULTURE

The application of the three theoretical paradigms of sociology to various topics will be highlighted in subsequent chapters. Making this application is simply a matter of revisiting the definition of the paradigm, isolating each of the key concepts, and then relating those key concepts to the topic. If we remember that the structural-functional paradigm is defined as a complex system whose parts work together to produce stability and solidarity, then the perspective of culture from that viewpoint would relate to how the various components of culture work together to meet human needs. It follows that every society has certain norms and values such as cooperation, efficiency, and rationality that enables a society to meet fundamental needs. Characteristic of all cultures are **cultural universals,** which are *traits that are part of every culture,* such as food preparation, laws, sexual mores, games and sports, and personal names, along with many other things. These traits help to stabilize a society; hence, they reinforce this perspective of culture.

FIGURE 5.4. Religious symbols as Cultural Universals.

The conflict approach sees society as an arena of inequality that generates conflict and change.[3] This paradigm pertains to how cultural norms and values reflect social inequality. For instance, certain American values such as individualism, competition, and material success benefit the affluent classes who have more resources, access to power, and better social connections. While the structural-functional paradigm ignores cultural diversity and downplays the importance of change in society, the social conflict approach understates the ways in which cultural patterns integrate society. Since culture is a broad and pervasive concept, it invites a macro perspective. It is best served by the two above mentioned models, much less so by the interactionist paradigm.

Since so much of who we are is based on culture, an understanding of the traits and components of one's culture is important to our collective self-understanding. Understanding other cultures is part of this self-understanding. As cultures begin to blend and fuse into a larger cultural pattern over time, the question of who we are as a people becomes deeper and more profound.

STUDY QUESTIONS

1. Discuss the ramifications of an emerging global culture. What are some of the positive and negative effects of this development?
2. Discuss some of the ways that American culture encourages inclusiveness and exclusiveness. Which is the more predominant in today's society and why?
3. What are some of the norms that govern student behavior? Discuss the distinction between institutional norms and the collective social norms of student interactions.

Figure Credits
Fig. 5.1a: Copyright © 2013 Depositphotos/Devon.
Fig. 5.1b: Copyright © 2015 Depositphotos/szefei.
Fig. 5.2: Copyright © 2010 Depositphotos/Paha_L.
Fig. 5.3: Source: https://la.wikipedia.org/wiki/Fasciculus:Vietnamdem.jpg.
Fig. 5.4: Copyright © 2014 Depositphotos/egal.

---

3 "Introduction to Sociology 204-2 (lecture 1)," Oregon State University, http://oregonstate.edu/instruct/soc204/plazad/lect1.htm.

CHAPTER SIX

Civilization & Society

SOCIETIES EXIST WITHIN a heritage of social norms, ethical values, traditional customs, belief systems, political systems, which we call civilizations. A **civilization** is defined as *the stage of human social development and organization that is considered most advanced.*[1] Hence, societies are evolving entities. If we survey the world, it is evident that there are numerous societies that are rudimentary, and others in various stages of evolutionary development. This is not to suggest that one society is better than another. Indeed, there is evidence to show that so-called primitive societies possess wisdom and knowledge that would benefit all societies, especially those considered the most evolved. Likewise, there is often a close relationship between the size and complexity of a society and its degree of social dysfunction. Nevertheless, all societies, large or small, simple or complex, comprise the entity of humanity.

However, the thrust of evolution is constantly upward despite the fact that this process is often very slow. Countries and regions of the world such as Japan, China and Western Europe (and its offshoots in North America and elsewhere) have a long history of institutional development, and possess a high degree of economic, political, and social sophistication. Consequently, they are by definition the most civilized.

Societies are responses to modified cultural ideals. Despite their level of development or self-awareness as a nation or a people, all societies have recognizable structures and functions. A **society** is *an aggregate of people living together in a more or less ordered community who share a common culture.* The community referred to can take many forms since it is defined by a particular territory, which may encompass the entire planet or a small sized group. Societies usually possess to some degree a dominant culture whose component ideals give purpose and shape to the character of the group. This is obvious in a homogeneous society, where the cultural patterns are roughly the same, but even in a multicultural society there is a core of values, norms, and beliefs that impact every community.

---

1 Oxford Living Dictionaries, s.v. "civilization," https://en.oxforddictionaries.com/definition/civilization.

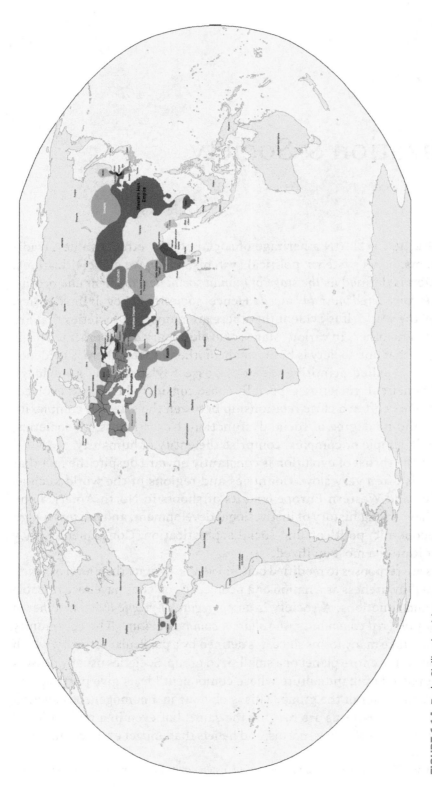

FIGURE 6.1A. Early Civilization Map.

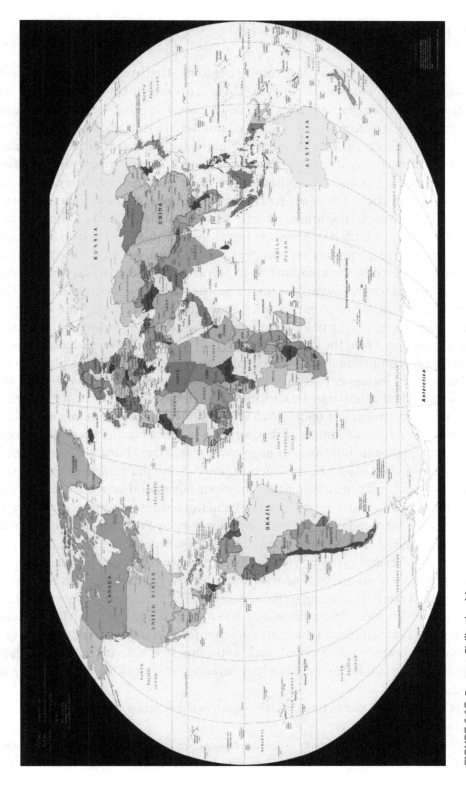

FIGURE 6.1B. Present Civilization Map.

COMPONENTS OF SOCIETY

The basic structure of a society rests on institutions. **Institutions** are *enduring and complex social structures that shape our lives.* There are five fundamental umbrella institutions: family, the economy, government, education, and religion. Of course, under each category there are numerous varieties of smaller institutions. For instance, your local bank, supermarket, or restaurant are primarily economic institutions although they may perform other institutional functions as well. There are certain characteristics of institutions. For one thing, they meet a basic human need. One could hardly imagine a society without any of the five basic institutions. Secondly, they endure for generations, even though they are constantly being modified. Think of the genealogy of your own family, which has developed over generations and centuries. Finally, institutions comprise a complex set of norms, values, statuses, and roles. Norms and values, which as we know are components of culture. **Statuses** are *positions one holds in society* such as teacher, lawyer, parent, or politician. **Roles** relate to *the functions, behaviors, or duties attached to each status.* From the perspective of the structural-functional paradigm, institutions have evolved to help groups and individuals to survive and function. From the conflict perspective, institutions reproduce inequality.

Societies are a composite of social groups. Groups not only involve a physical connection but also an interplay of feelings and minds. A **social group** *consists of two or more people who identify and interact with one another.* Basically, there are two types of groups. A **primary group** is *a small group whose members share personal and enduring relationships.*[2] An obvious example of this sort of group is a family. **Secondary groups** are *large and impersonal collections of people whose members pursue a specific goal or activity.* A college class would be one such example. Students come together to study a particular subject and even though they may know one another, their aim is to complete the course with a passing grade. Clearly, many groups combine characteristics of both. A sports team may closely bond its members, at the same time the purpose of the team is to enter into competition with other teams and to win games.

There are also several types of groups. An **aggregate** *consists of people in the same place who have little or no interaction or sense of identity.* A group of people waiting at a bus stop would constitute an aggregate. A **crowd** is *a temporary gathering of people who share a common focus of attention and who influence one another.*[3] The audience at a concert or a football game will come together for a short period of time to watch a performance or game and respond quickly to suggested activity such as applause, chanting, or other such behavior. Finally, a **category** is simply *a group of people who*

---

2   "Types of Social Groups," Lumen Learning, https://courses.lumenlearning.com/boundless-sociology/chapter/types-of-social-groups/.

3   Mimi Abramovitz, "Social Movements and Social Change," in *The Dynamics of Social Welfare Policy*, eds. Joel Blau and Mimi Abramovitz (Oxford University Press, 2010), 204.

FIGURE 6.2A. Primary Group.

FIGURE 6.2B. Secondary Group.

have the same status in common. Teachers, students, teammates, or roommates are categories that relate to college life.

More structured groups, meaning those that have clearly defined norms and values, constitute formal organizations. There are three kinds of organization. **Utilitarian organizations** are *those that provide some benefit or reward.* Any job or career where you are paid a wage or salary would so apply. A **Normative organization** is one which *provides a worthwhile experience or desirable goal.* While volunteer organizations offer services for which one is not paid, they may give someone a sense of purpose or well-being. Finally, a **coercive organization** *enforces involuntary membership.* A prison is an obvious example of this sort of organization.

EVOLVING CONSCIOUSNESS AND SOCIAL CHANGE

There are a number of theories as to how and why societies change. Fundamentally, social change comes about through the expansion of consciousness. Historical changes from ancient times to the medieval period, to early modern society, and later, modern and the post-modern world, have all been accompanied by changes in the way people think. However, until the last couple of centuries, such changes had, with some exceptions, a limited impact since only a very small percentage of the population was educated and open to new ideas. Hence, the response to the ideas that were generated took a long time to manifest.

Even a century ago, the United States was still a rural society where large numbers of people lived isolated lives and many children were not educated beyond the eighth grade. Prior to 1920, less than twenty percent of students completed high school. In 1869/70, only two percent of high school students graduated. By 2015–2016, the percentage of high school graduates was 84 percent. Over the past hundred years, we have become exposed to excessive amounts of information from sundry sources; consider the impact of the radio, motion pictures, television, and information technologies. As people become more mentally stimulated, they are more responsive to ideas, which in turn gives rise to new ideals, technologies, lifestyles, and communications, which speed up the pace of life. Therefore, we have a greater awareness of the society in which we live. The pressures brought on by an evolving consciousness has challenged existing institutions, which now find it increasingly difficult to meet the demands of the modern world. Consequently, the goal is to create new ways of thinking to accommodate the paradigm shifts that are taking place.

One sociologist who recognized the importance of ideas in bringing about social change was Max Weber (1865-1920). Weber coined the term **idealism** to explain *how human ideas shape society.* Concepts such as Protestantism, humanism, Marxism, democracy, among many others were used by Weber to *explain the essential qualities of a society.* These he called **ideal types**.

Weber explained how ideas bring about social change in light of two world views. He saw **tradition** in terms of *norms, values, and beliefs passed from generation to generation.* People in a traditional society tended to look backward for answers to current problems. Such societies often revered elders as the repositories of generational wisdom. Since traditional societies viewed events in the social world as beyond their control, especially catastrophes like floods, plagues, and famine, they often resorted to rituals, ceremonies, and so-called superstitions to mollify the gods or forces in nature.

On the other hand, a worldview based on **rationality** inclines people to see society as *a logical relation between means and ends.* The term **rationalization of society** refers to *the historical transition from a society based on tradition to one of rationality.* Implied by rationality is that problems can be resolved through a systematic approach employing human effort and ingenuity. Individuals, groups, and organizations thus set up social structures to create a division of labor to organize and carry out a specific function. If a community was stricken with a flood, for instance, residents in a rational society would instinctively organize into groups and be assigned a specific task to combat the problem. The flowchart of any organization reflects this division of labor. A rational social organization is characterized by specialized tasks, time-discipline, technical competence, and a degree of impersonality. Such a structure is known as a bureaucracy. When bureaucracies become too overgrown and complex to the point where they cease to be functional, they lead to a condition of alienation. Weber thought that this effect on those within the organization contributed to dehumanization.

TECHNOLOGY AND SOCIAL CHANGE

Since ideas are the basis for technology, they underscore a model put forth by theorist Gerhard Lenski, who argued that social change was brought about through transformations in technology. He suggested that in the course of human history there have been four major revolutions in technology that have ushered in a new society.

The oldest and now rarest society is the **hunter–gatherer society**, which consists of small bands of foragers who live off the land and use stone and wood tools. The first transformation in technology was the creation of the hoe and sickle and the ability to harvest seeds and irrigate fields, which led to the formation of **horticultural societies**, built around semi-permanent villages with a hierarchical social structure. Around the same time there arose **pastoral societies**, which were tribes of nomadic peoples that had learned to domesticate animals and moved from place to place depending on the food supply. These societies had rudimentary social structures including a chief, a religious leader, and others with a specified status. Both kinds of society numbered several hundred to a thousand or more members.

FIGURE 6.3A. Hunter/Gatherer Society.

The invention of animal-drawn farm implements that allowed for wide-scale cultivation of varieties of crops brought on **agricultural societies**. This second technological revolution employed millions of peasants on the land and also led to a complex division of labor that allowed for many non-agricultural occupations to develop. Tradesmen, merchants, craftsmen, blacksmiths, and small farmers sprang up within agrarian societies. Because far more food and other items produced exceeded the needs of a town or region, cities and empires emerged as trade and commerce spread all over the planet. Agrarian societies were dominant for over 6,000 years.

The use of machine power, at first steam and later oil and electricity, laid the basis for Lenski's third technological revolution known as the Industrial Revolution, ushering in an **industrial society**. The rise of mass production and mass-market economies led to extensive urbanization and the growth of even more complex institutions. Industrialization has also brought about specialization with a corresponding growth of diverse statuses and occupations. Likewise, industrial societies have generated great wealth and the emergence of the masses of people, hitherto ignored, as citizens in communities and nations. Technological knowledge, according to Lenski, has provided the basis for the most recent (fourth) revolution, or **post-industrial society**,

FIGURE 6.3B. Industrial Society.

predicated on information science based on computers, nanotechnologies, photonics, and robotics. Where this revolution will eventually lead is anyone's guess.

CLASS CONFLICT AND SOCIAL CHANGE

Perhaps the most important social and economic theorist in the nineteenth century was Karl Marx. He developed a theory of social change based on the conflict between social classes. Basic to Marx's model of society was that the technical and social processes of economic production were the catalyst for social transformation. He referred to economic forces as the infrastructure that characterized and determined the superstructure comprising the other social institutions along with cultural norms, values, and beliefs. Accordingly, each society was defined by **social class**, which is *the division of society based on social and economic status*. There are many classes in society, but for Marx there were essentially two classes: those who controlled the wealth of a society and owned the property, and those who supplied the labor. Accordingly, history was marked by **class conflict**, or *the tension and antagonism which exists in society due to competing socioeconomic interests and desires between people of different classes.*[4]

4   Charles Hurst, *Social Inequality: Forms, Causes, and Consequences* (Content Technologies, Inc., 2014).

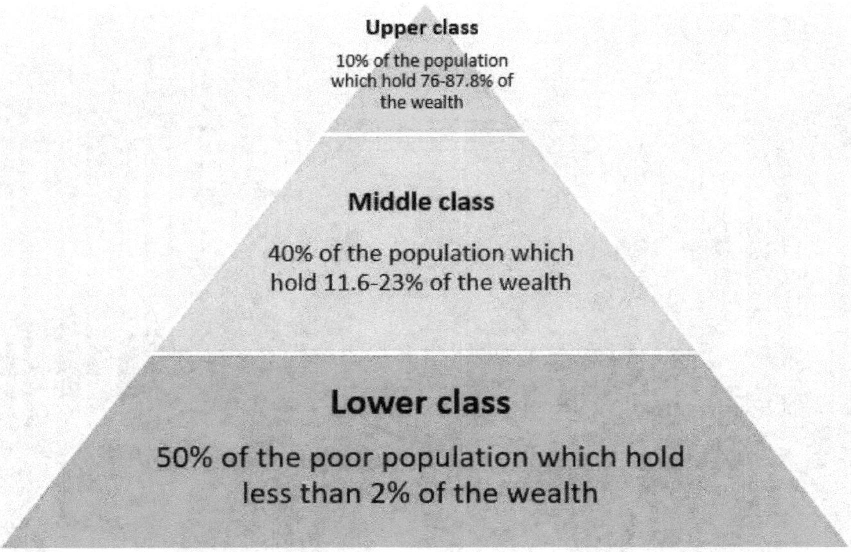

Upper class

10% of the population
which hold 76-87.8% of
the wealth

Middle class

40% of the population which
hold 11.6-23% of the wealth

Lower class

50% of the poor population which hold
less than 2% of the wealth

FIGURE 6.4. Different Social Classes.

Marx placed class conflict within a historical context starting with hunter-gatherer societies, which he referred to as primitive communism because they had no classes due to their small size and cohesion. As the economic structure changed, classes and class conflict appeared. Control of the means of production, in what Marx termed ancient society, fell into the hands of a small class of masters who exerted control over a massive number of slaves. The revolt of the underclass led to a feudal society in which a predominant peasant class labored and provided the economic resources for the nobility. With the coming of industrialization, a new class emerged out of the peasantry, which Marx called the proletarians. This class stood in opposition to the property-owning capitalist class. It was this last struggle which occurred during his lifetime that was the focus of Marx's analysis.

According to Marx, the scientific laws of economics, upon which capitalism and previous economic systems were based, forced workers to live at near-starvation wages. Initially, workers labored under the illusion of **false consciousness**, or *a way of thinking that prevents a person from perceiving the true nature of their social or economic situation*. For Marx, the industrial system contributed to his definition of alienation which was the experience of isolation resulting from a sense of powerlessness. Gradually, the proletariat developed **class consciousness**, which *is recognition on the part of the workers as part of a class in opposition to the capitalists and capitalism*. The recognition among workers of their common plight was the first step in engaging in political activity that would lead to revolution and the overthrow of the capitalist class. Marx's model encapsulated the conflict paradigm by which inequality leads to conflict and change.

FIGURE 6.5. Class Conflict.

STRUCTURE AND FUNCTION AS SOCIAL CHANGE

One of the major proponents of the structural-functional paradigm was sociologist Emile Durkheim. Unsurprisingly, he viewed society as the interplay between social structure and its consequent functions. Since social structure involves stable and recurrent patterns of social behavior, society is more than the individuals that compose it. Social structures are essentially **social facts**, which are *patterns of social behavior that have an objective reality beyond the lives of individuals*. A college course is a social fact that exists whether students show up for class or not. By the same token, crime is a social fact regardless of which individuals commit illegal acts. In both cases there exists patterns of behavior independent of those who participate in such activities.

Social structures have functions. In other words, social facts, which shape the behavior of individuals, help to shape the society as a whole. Hence, social facts are functional. Seen from another perspective, social facts as functions provide order to social situations and create stability that allows groups, organizations, and institutions to function properly.

Durkheim thought that social solidarity was maintained through a division of labor that involved a degree of interdependence of various tasks and occupations.

For instance, starting up a business requires interactions with banks, suppliers, government agencies, lawyers, and advertising outlets, among others. Durkheim differentiated between a pre-industrial and a modern society. Pre-industrial societies were based on what he called **mechanical solidarity** or *the social integration of members of a society who have common values and beliefs*. These common values and beliefs constitute a "collective conscience" that works internally in individual members to lead them to cooperate.[5] German sociologist and philosopher Ferdinand Tonnies called this kind of society a **Gemeinschaft,** *or a type of social organization by which people are related by kinship and tradition*.[6] An Amish community would be an example.

Modern societies were predicated on what Durkheim called **organic solidarity** or *social unity based on a division of labor that results in people depending on each other*. Organic solidarity relates more to industrial societies where social bonds are based on specialization and interdependence. Tonnies's term for this sort of society is **Gesellschaft**, which stood for *a social order whereby people come together on the basis of self-interest*. This form of social organization favors individualism and a diversity of norms, values, and beliefs.

Like Weber and Marx, Durkheim also believed that the social order produced alienation. He coined the term **anomie** to describe alienation as *a condition in which society provides little moral guidance*. Based on his study of suicide, Durkheim found that the least regulated people in society were the most likely to end their lives. His conclusions highlighted the power of norms and values underscoring social structures as the basis for a functional society.

STUDY QUESTIONS

1. Briefly discuss the theories of social change as presented by Gerhard Lenski, Karl Marx, Max Weber, and Emile Durkheim. How do Marx, Weber, and Durkheim view alienation as the result of this process?
2. What are some of the characteristics of a "civilized society" as opposed to one that is in an earlier stage of development?
3. To what extent does the size of a social group determine its function?

---

5 "Mechanical and organic solidarity," Editors of *Encyclopaedia Britannica*, February 9, 2010, https://www.britannica.com/topic/mechanical-and-organic-solidarity.
6 Carla G. Surratt, *The Internet and Social Change* (McFarland, 2001), 50.

Figure Credits

CHAPTER SEVEN

Socialization & The Life Cycle

AFTER EXPLORING THE macro topics of culture and society, our focus will now shift to the micro level as we investigate the life process known as socialization. **Socialization** is defined as *the lifelong learning process related to the discovery of oneself through learning one's culture.* This brings us back to the question of who are we, which is all about the self, or one's essential being. The term **being** refers to *the nature or essence of a person.* A human being relates to those traits that differentiate humans from animals. That said, **human nature** consists of *general psychological attributes and behavioral patterns shared by all humans.*

To understand how the self evolves over the course of the lifecycle, we must remember that there is a permanent self (soul), which is the product of many lifetimes of evolutionary experience, and the impermanent self (personality) that develops and gains knowledge within a single life. The nature–nurture debate, which has traditionally framed how sociologists view socialization, has some application to these two aspects of self. **Nature**, defined as *innate learning* pertains to those characteristics that one brings into life. Far from the limited perspective of innate learning being a purely fixed biological and physiological phenomenon, it can be taken to mean the knowledge and experience accumulated over many life cycles, whereas **nurture**, or *social learning*, can be seen as relating to personality development. Socialization can be explained in terms of psychological and social theories, which have references to both perspectives of self.

THEORIES OF PSYCHOLOGICAL SOCIALIZATION

One of the most important psychologists of the past century was Carl Jung (1875–1961). Jung's model outlined the various layers of self. The most recognizable was what he called the **collective consciousness**, which is our everyday awareness of the world around us based on information obtained through the senses. Below this threshold there is the **personal unconscious,** consisting of repressed memories, feelings, and fears that may lead to conditions of neurosis and psychosis. At a deeper level, there is the **collective unconscious** that responds to what Jung called archetypes, which are recurrent symbols or primal images that exist in the psychic atmosphere and can be universally conceived. Beyond the unconscious state, there is the **super consciousness,** which is psychic wholeness. This might be seen as representative of soul consciousness, although Jung never characterized it that way. What he did suggest is that humans possess a fundamental urge to overcome the dualities of their nature and achieve unity.

A more explicit illustration of the relationship between personality and soul can be found in the work of psychologist Roberto Assagioli (1888–1974). What Assagioli called **psychosynthesis** is the formation or reconstruction of the personality around a new center, which he referred to as the higher self, or the soul. Like Jung, Assagioli sees psychosynthesis as consisting of various layers of consciousness. In his model there are three states of unconsciousness: The **lower unconscious** directs and controls bodily functions; the **middle unconscious** which assimilates ordinary cognitive and imaginative faculties; and the **higher unconscious** through which we receive inspirations and altruistic urges. Then there is a field of consciousness that is part of the personality through which one is aware of the thoughts, feelings, images, and desires forming perceptions of the world around us. The **conscious self, or "I" self** is the point of pure self-awareness, or the center point of personal consciousness.

Beyond the conscious self, there is a permanent center known as the **higher self** that can only be realized through certain psychological methods, such as meditation. There is also a sphere, analogous to a membrane, which boundaries all these planes of consciousness, corresponding to Jung's collective unconscious. Psychological self-realization is achieved when the two perceived identities of self (the "I" self and higher self) merge into a unified sense of being, which we might refer to as soul awareness.

Whereas both Jung and Assagioli examined the various levels of consciousness culminating in a transpersonal or permanent self, other psychologists focused more specifically on the stages of human development within the life cycle. One such person was the Swiss psychologist Jean Piaget (1896–1980). Piaget was interested in how children learn, which led him to spend many years studying cognitive development in young people.

According to Piaget, children develop through four stages. The first is what he called the **sensorimotor stage**. It is during this period covering roughly the first two years of life that a child begins to experience the environment. This is a very tactile period in which the child gains knowledge though direct contact with their surroundings. The second stage he called the **preoperational stage**, which is the preschool age (2–7). At this point, the child learns rudimentary language and engages in social interaction. It is at this point where children exhibit very active imaginations. The **concrete operational stage** covers the period of childhood up to about age eleven.

Piaget's Stages of Cognitive Development

Stage	Age range	What happens at this stage?
Sensorimotor	0-2 years old	Coordination of senses with motor responses, sensory curiosity about the world. Language used for demands and cataloguing. Object permanence is developed.
Preoperational	2-7 years old	Symbolic thinking, use of proper syntax and grammar to express concepts. Imagination and intuition are strong, but complex abstract thoughts are still difficult. Conservation is developed.
Concrete Operational	7-11 years old	Concepts attached to concrete situations. Time, space, and quantity are understood and can be applied, but not as independent concepts.
Formal Operational	11 years old and older	Theoretical, hypothetical, and counterfactual thinking. Abstract logic and reasoning. Strategy and planning become possible. Concepts learned in one context can be applied to another.

The Psychology Notes Headquarters - https://www.PsychologyNotesHQ.com

FIGURE 7.1. Piaget's Stages of Cognitive Development.

During this period, the child develops language skills and begins the process of thinking logically albeit at a literal or concrete level. The final stage in Piaget's scheme is the **formal operational stage** which a child reaches around puberty. Here the child learns to reason abstractly and engage in hypothetical thinking. By the time one reaches adolescence, so Piaget thought, the basic apparatus of cognitive development had been achieved, which provided the structure for further learning.

Using a similar model, Lawrence Kohlberg developed a theory of how children undergo moral development. His scheme included three stages. Very young children learned moral behavior through what he called the **preconventional stage**. This involves the use of rewards and punishments to impose discipline since the child is only responsive to external stimuli. As a child becomes older, he or she grows into the **conventional stage**. By this time, the child has begun to internalize fundamental cultural norms and values, having learned that certain behaviors are either good or bad. This is a very literal understanding of morality. Children pass into the **postconventional stage** upon entering adolescence. It is at this point in life that one begins to think in terms of abstract principles, realizing that questions of morality are not absolute, and are often ambiguous or situational. Essentially, Kohlberg's theory of moral development can be overlapped with Piaget's stages of cognitive development.

Kohlberg's Theory

Level/Stage	Age Range	Description
I: Obedience/Punishment	Infancy	No difference between doing the right thing and avoiding punishment
I: Self-Interest	Pre-school	Interest shifts to rewards rather than punishment - effort is made to secure greatest benefit for oneself
II: Conformity and Interpersonal Accord	School-age	The "good boy/girl" level. Effort is made to secure approval and maintain friendly relations with others
II: Authority and Social Order	School-age	Orientation toward fixed rules. The purpose of morality is maintaining the social order. Interpersonal accord is expanded to include the entire society
III: Social Contract	Teens	Mutual benefit, reciprocity. Morally right and legally right are not always the same. Utilitarian rules that make life better for everyone
III: Universal Principles	Adulthood	Morality is based on principles that transcend mutual benefit.

The Psychology Notes Headquarters - http://www.PsychologyNotesHQ.com

FIGURE 7.2. Kohlberg's Stages of Moral Development.

While Piaget and Kohlberg saw socialization in terms of childhood development, Erik Erickson (1902–1994) saw it as a lifelong period of growth and challenges. His model is divided into eight stages:

Stage One—Infancy and the Challenge of Trust

Infancy is a time when a child needs to feel that the world is a safe place.

Stage Two—Toddlerhood and the Challenge of Autonomy

Up to age three the child needs to learn self-control and confidence in their sphere of activity.

Stage Three—The Challenge of Initiative

Preschool children need to confront the world beyond their home and engage with non-family members.

Stage Four—The Challenge of Industriousness

> School-age children need to widen their horizons, make friends with peers, engage in tasks, and feel proud of their accomplishments.

Stage Five—The Challenge of Identity

> Adolescents need to establish a sense of self and identity with others. Also, they need to get a sense of their own uniqueness.

Stage Six—The Challenge of Intimacy vs. Isolation

> Young adults need to be able to establish intimate relationships and to balance the need to bond with establishing a separate identity.

Stage Seven—The Challenge of Making a Contribution

> Adults in their mature years need to develop their careers or some form of livelihood and to balance their various commitments and responsibilities in life.

Stage Eight—The Challenges of Old Age

> People in the later years of life need to feel that their lives have been of value and they have made some mark on society.

According to Erickson, failure to meet the challenges at each stage of development creates problems that retard the growth of the individual. As with Piaget and Kohlberg, the stages that these theorists put forward are only rough guidelines as individuals evolve and mature at different rates.

THEORIES OF SOCIOLOGICAL SOCIALIZATION

Sociologists have tended to view socialization as a process of social learning. This stems from the inherent bias within sociology that tends to view human experience as the product of social forces acting upon individuals. While, as we have seen, this is not the whole story, there is no question that the self is shaped and molded by contact with the environment. Perhaps the best-known figure within this school of thought was George Herbert Mead (1863–1931). Mead defined the **self** as that *part of an individual's personality composed of self-awareness and self-image.*[1] What he meant by

---

1   John Bratton, Peter Sawchuk, Carolyn Forshaw, Militza Callinan, and Martin Corbett, "Personality," in *People, Work and Organisations*, eds. David Spicer and Hugh Lee (Palgrave Macmillan, 2014), 155.

FIGURE 7.3. Iraqi Boy Kicks Ball—Demonstration of George Herbert Mead's Play Stage.

this statement is that the self develops only through social experience. Mead coined the term **generalized other** to refer to *the widespread norms and values we use as references in evaluating others.* In other words, our personal set of rules and standards is a filter through our consciousness by which we conceptualize and judge the behavior of others.

Mead, like Piaget and Kohlberg, also put forth a model of developmental stages, but he put the focus on social learning. Accordingly, infants passed through what Mead called the **preparatory stage** in which the child sees no distinction between the self and others and is totally self-absorbed. Learning takes place through observation of the surrounding environment. The **play stage** is the developmental period for preschool children. At this stage, the child learns to distinguish between the self and others, and begins to imitate others by assuming different roles. The child may pick up the mannerisms of his or her parents, for instance. Older children move on to the **game stage** where they enter into activities that require an understanding of multiple roles. Whether it is a simple game or sports, one has to know the functions and activities of other participants in order to satisfactorily perform their role.

Another theorist, Charles Horton Cooley, put forth the idea of the **looking-glass self,** which posited that *self-image is based on how we think other people see us.* It follows that we constantly perceive signals or impressions of self from others. These impressions are then internalized and often magnified, which form a person's conception of self. This sense of self then contributes to behavioral patterns directed towards other groups or individuals. Often, of course, these initial impressions may be misinterpreted, which is the cause of much confusion and dis-harmony in social relations. Obviously, the looking-glass self changes as one becomes older and more mature. The more one understands the dynamics of self, the better able are they to interpret the reactions from others.

Furthermore, there are two aspects of self: The **I self** and the **me self.** The I self is the active self, which is the projection of one's thoughts and behavior. "I am going to the store," or "I love you," are two such examples. The me self is the passive self, and relates to the self as the recipient of something. "Give me the book," or "Why don't you like me?" fall into this category.

SOCIALIZATION AND THE LIFE CYCLE

A normal life consists of various stages of being with a number of transition points. These stages form a cycle of experience that can be divided into periods of seven years. These would include infancy and early childhood up to age seven, later childhood and early adolescence up to age fourteen, adolescence to age twenty-one, then six cycles of adulthood up to age sixty-three, followed by several more cycles to the end of one's life. Of course, there are other ways to divide the life cycle and in terms of life experiences, however, they can only be approximations.

The stages of transition are marked by crisis points. Puberty, or the emergence of sexual maturity, the transition into adulthood between the ages of eighteen and twenty-one, a crisis of self-identification that often takes place between the late twenties and early thirties, and much later the crisis brought on by retirement and the entry into senior citizenhood.

Throughout the life cycle, one is confronted with various agents of socialization that influence and modify thought and social behavior. The family, naturally is the singular most important influence, particularly in the younger years when contact with parents and siblings is dominant. As a child enters school and expands his or her circle of contacts, peers and peer groups assume growing importance on attitudes and behavior. This assumes even greater importance during the adolescent years. Beyond personal contacts, there is the overwhelming importance of interactive social media and other mass media that shape and mold public opinion. According to CNN digital correspondent Kelly Wallace, teens spend nine hours a day consuming media which is roughly three hours more than they spend in school. A thirteen-year-old may click on to social media one hundred times a day. While people may bring into the world lifetimes of encapsulated experiences, the impact on them by agents of socialization within society today has never been greater.

TOTAL INSTITUTION & RESOCIALIZATION

Certain groups of people, *either voluntarily or involuntarily, are isolated from society and manipulated by administrative staff* in what is called a **total institution**. Monks or members of a closed religious order and members of the armed forces are examples of voluntary isolation in such institutions, prisoners are the obvious examples of the latter.

The purpose of a total institution is **re-socialization**, which aims to *radically alter an inmate's thoughts and behavioral patterns through re-structuring their environment*. In some instances, as in prisons, the environment may contribute more to the re-socialization of an inmate than the intended goal of making them fit to live in society. In any case, re-socialization may have a long-lasting impact, beyond the time spent within the total institution.

Socialization is obviously functional to the well-being of a society, which is how it would be perceived by a structural-functional theorist. Conversely, a conflict theorist would argue that one is often socialized to patterns of inequality and rankings in society, which would impact one's perception of self. While at its root socialization is about self-awareness, this evolving sense of consciousness is central to how societies grow and develop.

STUDY QUESTIONS

1. Discuss socialization with respect to the nature-nurture question regarding the theories of Roberto Assagioli, Jean Piaget, and George Herbert Mead. Which model do you find the most convincing? Explain why.

2. Which model, George Herbert Mead's generalized other or Charles Cooley's looking-glass self, do you think best explains how we see ourselves from a sociological perspective? Explain why.

3. Discuss the various agents of socialization as they impact your life. Which ones would you say exert the greatest influence, and why?

Figure Credits

CHAPTER EIGHT

The Social Construction of Reality

WHAT IS REALITY? There is no clear answer to this question since reality is based upon one's level of consciousness. So defined, **reality** is *the world or the state of things as they actually exist, as opposed to an idealistic or notional idea of them.*[1] It may be argued that "a state of things as they actually exist" can be understood only by the soul, otherwise reality is just a limited perception of whatever point in consciousness one's attention is focused on. This, of course, frequently changes as we interact with the environment, which evokes various emotions, memories, and thoughts.

Reality is also a social phenomenon based on collective perceptions as to the way things appear to be. A common sense view of reality may be true or false, which is why an attitude of critical thinking is so important. As Peter Berger pointed out (Chapter One), the wisdom of sociology is that "things are not what they seem." In other words, social reality has many layers of meaning, and as each new layer is discovered, it changes our perception of the whole.[2] The approach to studying interactions in everyday life, favored by sociologists, is to step back and objectively observe what is going on in one's immediate environment. At the same time, it is necessary to be aware that behavioral patterns often mask a hidden layer of reality that may be more telling than what one sees. That will be the focus of this chapter.

STATUSES AND ROLES

We briefly mentioned the terms status and roles in Chapter Six, but more elaboration is necessary since they are fundamental as to understanding social

---

1 Oxford Living Dictionaries, s.v. "reality," https://en.oxforddictionaries.com/definition/reality.

2 Peter L. Berger, *Invitation to Sociology: A Humanistic Perspective* (Anchor Books, 1963), 1–24, https://www.csustan.edu/sociology/why-study-sociology.

interaction. Status, as we know, is a social position a person occupies. A person may have an **ascribed status**, which is *a status one inherits at birth*. Examples would be one's race, ethnicity, or rank in society based upon the status of one's parents. **Achieved status** *is a status that one acquires through their own efforts or state of being*. Becoming a teenager or passing exams to achieve a college degree constitutes a status that is achieved. The collection of *all the statuses a person holds* constitutes a **status set**. In some cases, one particular status, like being a nation's president or prime minister, outshines all other statuses a person may have. This is called a **master status**.

FIGURE 8.1. High School Classroom—Performing the Student Role.

There are also various categories of roles. Roles are expected behaviors attached to each status. Busy people are often confronted with performing numerous roles simultaneously, which overlap with one another. For instance, a full-time student who is engaged in extra-curricular activities and works part-time would most likely experience **role conflict.** By the same token, when there is tension between roles connected to a particular status, a person would undergo **role strain**. Such would be the case of a politician who must balance a multitude of personal and public responsibilities. When a person leaves a job, a marriage, or some other status, that is known as **role exit.**

THE SOCIAL CONSTRUCTION OF REALITY

From a sociological perspective, people shape their reality through social interaction. *The study of how individuals make sense of their everyday surroundings* is called **ethnomethodology.** In the first place, we must remember that there are rules (norms) that govern every social situation so that understanding these rules, which often occurs by breaking them, makes one realize the extent to which social structures govern human behavior. One example is "small talk." When people engage each other in conversation there is usually preliminary chatter, such as "How are you?" "I am fine." "What's up?" and then perhaps some aimless talk about the weather. It is not that these are serious concerns, but they are an attempt to "break the ice" so as to get to a more meaningful dialogue. Hence, small talk has a functional use. People also tend to treat appearances as real. If you are stopped by a policeman, you naturally assume that the person in uniform is a cop, even though, hypothetically, it could be anyone masquerading as such. Our approach to the environment is conditioned by a multitude of assumptions and internalized social patterns that help us to navigate through complex interactions.

Another way we make sense of our surroundings is by distinguishing between imagined and actual situations. It is true to say that our perceptions shape our reality. William Isaac Thomas (1863–1947) and Dorothy Swaine Thomas (1899–1977) formulated a theorem, stating *"If men define situations as real, they are real in their consequences."* This **Thomas theorem** in other words is how the interpretation of a situation leads to action. This interpretation is not objective. Actions are affected by subjective perceptions of situations. Whether there is even a correct interpretation is not important for the purposes of helping guide individuals' behavior.[3] For example, if a person was afraid to walk down a dark street alone at night, they may hail a taxi or take some other evasive route. Hence, perception determines action. Carrying this theory further, sociologist Robert Merton put forward the idea of a **self-fulfilling prophecy** which is *if something is defined as real and people act accordingly, then what was defined may turn out to be real.* If a person is praised for being a model student, that might drive said person to study harder so as to live up to that expectation.

Similarly, **frames** are *definitions and expectations of an interactive episode.* We approach many social situations with certain unstated expectations. For instance,

---

3   Pierpalo Donati, Relational Sociology: A New Paradigm for the Social Sciences (New York: Routledge, 2010).

suppose you go to the mall to buy an article of clothing. When approaching the sales-person/cashier with your purchase, you would expect the person to be knowledgeable about the products they are selling, to answer your questions politely, to wait on people in order, and to charge you the correct amount for your purchase. If the person violated any of these norms, this may change your perception of the interaction and behavior accordingly.

FIGURE 8.2. Theatrical Performance at Western College.

On a larger scale, we carry around with us **frames of reference**, which are *often unconscious mental structures that affect the way we perceive the social world.* A police-man would probably use as a frame of reference the need to maintain public order, a school teacher would be motivated by the importance of education, and a nurse by the ideal of promoting health. These frames of reference are attributes of consciousness born of general principles.

Dramaturgical Analysis

Media of various sorts (theatre, movies, TV, social media) mirror human society past, present, and imaginatively, the future. Whereas images of the social world conveyed through the media tend to be thematic, they do offer a structure to depict and understand society. If we explore a theatrical performance, for instance, we can see the action in terms of status and roles. Status refers to the part one plays, whereas the role relates to the script. Translated into everyday life, we take on a status and perform a role in every social situation in which we find ourselves, whether as a student, team player, family member, or something else.

In the great theatre of life, we consciously, or unconsciously, present ourselves in certain ways. Erving Goffman (1922–1982), who developed the idea of dramaturgical analysis, believed that people in social situations seek to present themselves in some positive fashion so as to avoid embarrassment or some negative reaction. This is done in a number of ways. Individuals often manipulate scenes so as to create desired impressions. Business people in a managerial meeting may position themselves around a table so as to be noticed by their boss, or not, as the case may be. Impression management relates to all aspects of a person's demeanor. Think about going on a job interview or a date. Special attention would no doubt be given to one's appearance, the language used, and the various forms of body language so as to present oneself in the most favorable light.

Two other terms that relate to presentation of self are **line**, or *verbal and non-verbal acts used to express an image of oneself,* and **face,** which is *the role or image one claims for themselves.* Picture a salesperson trying to make a sale. He or she will aim to be as friendly as possible in order to make a positive impression so as to support the spin they are putting on their service or product. If they are met with a negative response from a customer or prospective client, the person making the pitch will necessarily alter their approach in order to save face. People often store within

FIGURE 8.3. Long-haired Woman Laughing.

themselves a number of **defensive practices**, which are *techniques to safeguard their created impressions*. These techniques vary according to the situation, and are usually honed through life experiences.

A further aspect of dramaturgical analysis can be termed front stage/back stage. This has some relation to public and private space. Imagine a fine restaurant. The dining area (front space) is quiet, with perhaps some soft background music. The wait staff are very attentive and the whole atmosphere has a serene and pleasant quality. The kitchen area (backstage) is quite different. There is much noise and confusion, with orders being shouted out and a considerable amount of commotion. Obviously, a theatre would have a similar dynamic.

Non-Verbal Communication

Communication is not only discourse but involves non-verbal communication. **Non-verbal communication** is about *using body movements, gestures, and facial expressions that convey meaning either intentionally or non-intentionally*. This can be summed up in the word **demeanor**, which is *expression of general conduct*. There are many predictable reactions to one's demeanor. **Use of space** is one example. Americans instinctively seek to maintain a distance from people they do not know, particularly in crowded circumstances. People in a crowded elevator, for instance, will feel uncomfortable and often avert their eyes from others to minimize contact. In other societies, people may have a different sense of space. By the same token, **staring** often makes people feel very uncomfortable and is generally considered rude. **Smiling** may invite a similar reaction from others. Why is this so? It might be argued that smiling at someone puts them on the spot, so a return smile is a way of presenting oneself in the most favorable light. **Touching** others carries with it many signals. It may be a way of establishing intimacy, or a desire to directly communicate in a positive manner. On the other hand, it may carry an inappropriate message, like being perceived as a form of sexual harassment or a display of power that is unwelcome.

Body language can mask deception. When placed in an awkward situation, our body language may belie an excuse or explanation. A person caught telling a lie may show signs of nervousness like fidgeting or looking embarrassed, while trying to give an unconvincing account of themselves. The term **idealization** refers to *performances that tend to idealize one's intentions*. A professor, when confronted with a question he or she does not know, may try to wing an answer so as to cover up a lack of knowledge.

Embarrassment refers to *slip-ups in our personal performance*. If at the dinner table with guests you accidently spill a dish of food into somebody's lap, that is clearly an embarrassing situation. Likewise, if someone at the table piped up saying that the dish was too hot or that this had happened to them before, that person would be expressing **tact** by *helping the embarrassed person to save-face*.

Playing with Reality

Words often have different meanings depending on how they are spoken and in what manner. This refers to latent and manifest meanings. A **manifest meaning** relates to *exactly to what is said*. Saying "thank you" upon receipt of a kind gesture would be a literal and appropriate response. **Latent meanings** refer *to additional assumptions or meanings of words*. Sarcasm is a good example. If someone steps on your foot and you reply "thanks," you are clearly conveying the opposite meaning from the literal intent of the word.

Another way by which people "play with reality" is through humor. **Humor** is defined as *a contrast between two incongruous realities*. Sometimes it involves words that have a double meaning.

> Sam: Joe, did you know that I am having a little affair?
> Joe: That's great Sam, who is catering it?

Humor also varies from country to country and is culturally defined, often playing off stereotypes. This is because countries have certain real or assumed characteristics, which are widely recognized. Finnish people are generally seen as being taciturn, Scottish people are perceived as tight with their money, French people are sensuous and romantic, Americans are brash and materialistic. Like all stereotypes, these characterizations are somewhat bogus in that they assume all people in a given country are the same. Nevertheless, they have a grain of truth and provide a basis for humor.

Humor relates to the three paradigms of sociology. From a **structural-functional perspective**, humor can act as a safety valve that releases social pressure. Imagine a room full of angry and uptight people. Someone then cracks a funny joke and everyone laughs. Afterward, everyone is much more at ease. On the other hand, humor can be a way of putting down minorities and marginalized groups, as in the case of Polish jokes, dumb blonde jokes, or jokes about one's weight, appearance, or physical condition. This would illustrate humor from a **conflict perspective**. In the course of general conversation, humor plays an important role in facilitating communication. It therefore is central to human interaction, which is the essence of the **interactionist perspective**.

STUDY QUESTIONS

1. Using sociological terminology as much as possible, discuss a social experience you have had in terms of dramaturgical analysis. In what way did one's presentation of self enter into this performance?
2. Discuss some of the ways body language can reveal deception.
3. Apply the Thomas Theorem to a social situation you have experienced, and explain your observations of that experience.

Figure Credits

Unit III

Social Differentiations

IT IS THE job of the sociologist to clarify not only what humanity has in common but how human beings and societies can be divided and distinguished by certain categories and traits. Chapters Nine through Twelve explore some of these distinguishing characteristics. All societies, to a greater or lesser degree, are stratified into different classes based on an assortment of criteria, which may include income, wealth, job status, level of education, ancestry, or any of a number of other things. Other demarcations include race, ethnicity, and gender. These characteristics are to large extent social creations that often subordinate one group within each of these categories to the power and authority of another group. The distinctiveness of these demarcations is determined by their historical development, reflecting changes in consciousness over time. Crime and deviance are other factors that are distinguishing characteristics within a society. The need for social control and the maintenance of certain moral and ethical standards require distinctions between acceptable and unacceptable behaviors that relate also to the use of social power by those in authority. In a similar manner, all societies need to regulate human passions, often expressed through sexual behavior. Sex is subject to changing attitudes that impact the values and norms of a society.

CHAPTER NINE

Stratification and Social Class

WHAT POSITION DO you hold within the social order? Contrary to popular opinion, the veneer of equality and social leveling in the United States belies the fact that American society has a pronounced social hierarchy. All societies divide themselves into a system of ranking. While there are many measures that can be employed to indicate stratification, they are mostly the effects of standards used to define social categories. Standards refer to a level of quality or attainment. Values are culturally defined standards, and as such they are based on perceptions of the wider world. Perceptions, as we have seen, are based on one's level of consciousness. Thus, stratification and social class are subjectively referring to the consciousness of how one thinks or feels about themselves and others. Furthermore, consciousness underscores a person's demeanor and thought processes that determine expression and patterns of behavior. Some of the subtle aspects of social class include speech, grammar, diction, emotional expression, the character of one's associates, and the assertion of inherited family patterns.

Since we are assuming that people have lived previous lives, it follows that structures of stratification are innate to the individual. This suggests that even though the idea of hierarchy may outwardly appear disagreeable to some, and may contradict cultural norms, it is a subjective fact that underscores all manner of relationships. The pervasiveness of social stratification is a reaffirmation of how we instinctively respond to the world around us whether we are conscious of this fact or not.

From a sociological perspective, however, stratification is a social creation that involves the objective ordering of people by social class. It is a way of seeing the general in the particular that helps sociologists make sense of society. In terms of being a social product, one is often defined by factors such as income and wealth, occupational prestige, the level of education, the exercise of power and authority, residential stratification, and so forth. Accordingly, **social stratification** is defined as *a system by which a society ranks categories* *of people in a hierarchy.*[1] **Social class** has a more limited definition as *the division of society based on social and economic factors*, however, as social constructions the understanding of class changes as social consciousness evolves.

SOCIAL FOUNDATIONS OF INEQUALITY

There are several characteristics that determine the nature of social stratification and class. The first is that they cut across numerous generations. A **generation** is *the term of years, roughly 30 among human beings, accepted as the average period between the birth of parents and the birth of their offspring.*[2] If you were to trace your family tree as far back as possible, you would find that your ancestors fit into a pattern of social stratification, even if it was different from your own.

Social stratification and social class are also impacted by social mobility. **Social mobility** is *shifting from one social status to another, commonly to a status that is either higher or lower.* For example, a professor whose parents were day laborers would have achieved upward social mobility. Likewise, a person of means who loses his or her money and social position and becomes a pauper would clearly represent downward social mobility. One of the national myths in American society is that social mobility is very fluid and stories of "rags-to-riches" are commonly believed. In fact, upward mobility over generations varies only slightly, especially true in recent decades. Social mobility often has a lot to do with figuring out complex social cues, or folkways, that give one the veneer of status. This is referred to as class-passing.

There are two forms of social mobility. **Intragenerational social mobility** involves *a change in social position within one's life*time. A person who goes from being a handyman to an engineer would exemplify this form of social mobility. **Intergenerational social mobility** concerns *a change in social position in relation to one's parents.* A child who achieves an advanced degree in college, surpassing their parents, who went no further than high school, would characterize intergenerational social mobility.

Needless to say, social stratification and class are universal, although they vary in terms of time and place. Hunter-gatherer societies (mentioned in Chapter Six), due to the small size of their social group, come the closest to a classless society but they are quite rare. In Great Britain, at least until recently, class was considered a form of national identity, whereas the United States has tended to pretend that class does not exist. The now defunct Soviet Union maintained that it had eliminated social classes, yet it possessed a hierarchy with an elite class.

---

1 "Stratification and Conflict," Study.com, https://study.com/academy/lesson/social-stratification-definition-theories-examples.html.

2 Dictionary.com, s.v. "generation," https://www.dictionary.com/browse/generation.

Social stratification and class are supported by widely held beliefs known as ideologies. **Ideologies** are *cultural beliefs that justify particular social arrangements, often patterns of social inequality.*[3] There are many examples of ideologies that govern the way people think about politics, economics, and social relationships. The idea that "everyone should have equal opportunity" or "people who work are entitled to more resources than those who do not work" stand as examples of commonly held ideologies. The importance of ideologies, particularly if they gain widespread acceptance, is that they often bring about social change, which accounts for the fact that stratification and class are not fixed structures but are mutable and evolve over time as the consciousness of a people change.

CASTE AND CLASS SYSTEMS

Two widely distinct systems of social stratification are those predicated on caste and class. A **caste** is *a type of social stratification that is founded exclusively on ascription, or birth.* A **class** is *a form of social stratification predicated on both ascription and individual achievement.* Caste-based societies provide for no upward social mobility since one's place at birth is their social position for life. As such, caste boundaries are very clear and are defined by dress, occupation, level of education, and other such factors relevant to a particular caste. At the same time, caste awareness is universally understood, and everyone knows their position on the social scale. African Americans during the period of segregation in the United States could have been considered a caste based on race since they were trapped within a racially defined category.

Social class is much more fluid, meaning that one can move up or down the social scale. Unlike a caste system that is predicated on inherited criteria, a class system highlights one's abilities and achievements. In a class-based society, recognition of one's status is often unclear. Modern western societies that have achieved a fair degree of economic growth and social mobility are often less aware and concerned about class than are more traditional societies. *Social relations in a class-based society are usually inclusive, involving interactions of people from different social, religious, economic, and ethnic back grounds.* This **exogamous** form of social relations contrasts with **endogamous** types of relations, characteristic of caste systems, in which *contacts between individuals exist almost entirely within their social group.*

---

3 "The Ideology of Inequality," Pace University, https://www.pace.edu/emplibrary/VP-TheIdeology-ofInequalityrevised2-Hugh_J_Scott.pdf.

FIGURE 9.1. Canal Street, New Orleans–Two Men of a Different Class.

SOCIAL MOBILITY AND STATUS CONSISTENCY

Since there are numerous indicators used to measure one's position in society, the grouping of these measures is called **socioeconomic status,** which is *the composite ranking based on various dimensions of social inequality.* Such dimensions of social inequality include **income**, which is *earnings derived from work or investments*, **wealth**, which is *the total values of money and all other assets minus debts*, **occupational prestige**, or *the social value placed on a given job or occupation*, and **schooling**, which is *the amount of formal education one has received.* These factors and others often pertain to the amount of social power one holds in society.

    Status consistency refers to *the degree of consistency across the various categories of social inequality.* For instance, if a person possessed a six-figure income, owned considerable amounts of property, had an advanced level of education, lived in the best part of town, and held the status of a company president, one could say that he or she had a high level of status consistency. The opposite would be true if all these indicators consistently pointed to a low status. To a large extent, however, people possess status inconsistency. For instance, a person from a middle-class background with a college education may be employed in a useful but low-paying job with few tangible assets. Status consistency, or inconsistency, is closely tied to social mobility since over the course of one's life there are constant adjustments as people change occupations, further careers, and experience the ups and downs of life experience.

THEORETICAL APPROACHES TO SOCIAL STRATIFICATION AND CLASS

The structural-functional perspective of social stratification is contained in a theory put forward by sociologists Kingsley Davis and Wilbert Moore, known as the **Davis-Moore thesis.** It states that *social stratification can be beneficial to the operation of society*.[4] Since stratification is about social hierarchies, one could argue that it imposes standards of achievement, fosters meritocracies, and engenders competition to ensure that groups and institutions function at a high level of capability. Moreover, stratification, by creating a system of rewards, ensures that needed positions are filled through inducements such as large salaries, fringe benefits, and high occupational status.

The critique of the Davis-Moore thesis comes from the conflict perspective which argues that social stratification creates inequality that results in social harm. Unlike the structural-functional approach that views society as a relatively level playing field, conflict theorists assume that a stratified society gives advantages to some and not others, thus denying many people the opportunity to develop and express their unique talents and abilities. Also, rewards in a market-based society are not necessarily predicated on social value. One might argue that the social benefit of a movie star or a highly-paid professional athlete does not exceed that of a much less-paid school teacher, businessperson, or a first-responder. On a broader scale the inequality gap between rich and poor is at the root of many social problems, not the least of which is lower social mobility.

SOCIAL CLASS AND POVERTY

If you were asked to define yourself in class terms, the question may give you pause. Like many people, you might answer that you are middle-class, since it is widely believed that in the United States the majority fall into what one writer called "the imperial middle." However, this is not the case. Studies have shown that less than

---

4   R.P. Pathak, *Education in the Emerging India* (New Delhi: Atlantic Publishers & Dist., 2007).

half the population can be defined as middle-class with slightly more falling within the classifications of working class, working poor, or the under-class. At the top of the pile are the very rich who constitute approximately one percent of the population, and whose economic worth is greater than the bottom ninety percent. A prime factor determining one's position on the social scale is education.

FIGURE 9.2. Migrant Mother.

One might ask why in the richest country in the world is there so much economic inequality and insecurity? While there is no single answer to this question, the system of private free-market capitalism that exists in the United States, with minimal protections for its most vulnerable citizens, would appear to be an obvious reason. Since economic power is usually equated with social and political power, it would seem that the indifference to class in the United States masks a distinct class system that favors those at the top. The fact that the income levels for the top five percent has grown at a much faster rate than those further down the social scale attests to a widening economic differential in American society.

SOCIAL CAUSES AND EFFECTS OF POVERTY

While poverty may be thought of by some as personal troubles, such as the inability of poor people to make rational financial choices, it is largely a social issue. The loss of income, or insufficient income due to unforeseen crises such as divorce, the termination of employment, catastrophic health matters, or the result of natural disasters is often the road to poverty. Individuals, like countries, share the same problem, meaning that it is hard for those with few resources to acquire greater resources.

The effects of poverty can be personally devastating, resulting in greater stress, family discord and violence, drug and alcohol abuse, and mental health issues. Poverty can also exacerbate social issues such as increases in property crime, homelessness, neighborhood deterioration, and the draining of public resources. A climb in the rate of poverty may result in a decline in consumer spending and a reduced tax base that can affect the economy as a whole.

Poverty can be assessed in quantitative and qualitative terms. There are various objective measures of poverty used by governments and other organizations, for example the poverty line and standard of living rates, to determine the degree and extent of poverty. Qualitative measures relate to quality of life issues pertaining to how poverty affects the social environment, its impact upon the nature of personal interactions, and the extent of opportunities afforded to poor people who often lack vital resources.

WHO ARE THE POOR?

There are essentially two sorts of poverty, **absolute poverty**, which is *poverty that is life-threatening,* and **relative poverty**, *which is the lack of resources by some people in relation to those who have more resources.* Absolute poverty is commonly found in the poorest regions of the planet where there is mass starvation and an inability to provide for one's basic needs. Relative poverty exists in most countries and is measured by the inability of families and individuals to maintain an adequate level of existence in relation to those who possess more resources. According to the US Census Bureau, approximately 43.1 million people, or 13.5% of the American population live in relative poverty.

The largest category of poor, not surprisingly, are children since they are nonproductive and rely on the resources of parents or others. The share of children in the United States living in relative poverty is, according to the OECD database, one of the highest in the world. By far, the vast amount of poverty is found in single-parent families, the majority of which are headed by women. Sociologists have coined the term **feminization of poverty**, referring to *a phenomenon in which women represent a disproportionate percentage of the world's poor.* This trend is not only a consequence of lack of income, but also of lack of opportunities due to gender biases and fixed gender roles in some societies.[5] In terms of race, the majority of poor are white people, although the percentage of minorities in poverty is higher.

EXPLAINING POVERTY

The reasons why people are poor relate to our theoretical models. According to the structural-functional model, poverty is an individual matter, and is the result of personal choices. This **blame-the-poor** perspective claims that *the poor are responsible for*

---

5 "Poverty," Lumen Learning, https://courses.lumenlearning.com/boundless-sociology/chapter/poverty/.

their own poverty, with the assumption being that society is composed of individuals who pursue their own interests.

The conflict model assumes that individuals are the product of society. The so-called **blame society** perspective assumes that *poverty is largely due to social forces that are beyond a person's control.* The assumption here is that people often become poor as the result of a health crisis, a natural disaster, the loss of income, or some other life crisis.

Whereas the blame-the-poor and blame-society explanations concern how people become poor, the third perspective, based on the interactive model, focusses on the **culture of poverty.** Accordingly, *poverty occurs in cycles and is learned behavior that passes from one generation to the next.* People caught within a culture of poverty have very little sense of why they are poor. It assumes that poverty, like other aspects of culture, has its own norms, values, and beliefs that are reinforcing over generations. This perspective explains why the problem of poverty often defies solutions aimed at eradicating its causes and enabling people to function better in society.

In the final analysis, poverty is a matter of perception, or consciousness that may be at odds with social definitions. A well-to-do family experiencing a decline in income, causing a reduction in their standard of living, may perceive themselves as poor when by all objective assessments they are doing quite well. Likewise, a person may live on limited resources yet feel rich in other respects. As stated in the beginning of this chapter, stratification and social class are subjective perceptions of consciousness that relate to how one thinks or feels about themselves and others. It could be argued that if everyone was given the same amount of money, within a short period of time some would end up rich, while others would possess few, if any, resources. It all comes down to an awareness of how wealth is used, its purpose, and possibilities.

STUDY QUESTIONS

1. Specifically describe your own family's social class taking account of education, income, wealth, occupational status, and ascription.
2. Drawing upon the three theoretical models for explaining poverty, which explanation, after discussing all three, do you find to be the most reasonable and why?
3. Do you think the Davis–Moore Thesis is a valid perspective for explaining social stratification in the United States? Why, or why not?

Figure Credits

CHAPTER TEN

Social and Historical Demarcations: Race, Ethnicity, Gender

FROM THE PLANE of the soul, distinctions that divide humanity into categories of race, ethnicity, gender, or any other grouping do not exist. It is only when consciousness is focused on the lower concrete mind, with its capacity to classify, grade, and designate are people grouped according to some imposed criteria. Likewise, when such groups are aggregated by feelings and assorted emotions, one's view of the world becomes easily distorted through a range of glamours and illusions. Consciousness when overshadowed by fear, anger, contempt, and numerous complementary emotions results in a condition of irrationality and the loss of one's critical faculties. The result is often some form of prejudice, which is a preconceived opinion that is not based on reason or actual experience.

DEFINITIONS OF PREJUDICE AND DISCRIMINATION

Prejudice is defined as *a rigid and irrational generalization about a group of people.* When *prejudices are carried out into some form of action that is detrimental to groups and individuals,* the result is **discrimination.** *When discrimination is tolerated or supported by the norms and values of formal groups and organizations,* you have **institutional discrimination.** In American society, race, ethnicity, and to some extent gender are prime factors that evoke prejudice and discrimination. Race, ethnicity, as well as gender are socially created concepts that have meaning within various societies, although they may be interpreted differently from place to place. **Race** is understood as *biologically transmitted traits defined as socially significant.* It is important to remember that technically race is a non-existent category insofar as all people, regardless of distinctions, belong to only one race—the human race. **Ethnicity** refers to *shared cultural practices, perspectives, and distinctions that set apart one group*

FIGURE 10.1. Placard- Racism is Never Justified.

of people from another. In other words, having a shared cultural heritage. The most common characteristics distinguishing various ethnic groups are ancestry, a sense of history, language, religion, and intangible rules and values.[1] **Gender** refers to *the social and cultural differences that relate to the state of being male or female.*

Whereas prejudice and discrimination pertain to persons within all three of the above categories, there are considerable differences as to how these attitudes and actions are applied and experienced. **Racism,** so defined, is *prejudice, discrimination, or antagonism directed against someone of a different race based on the belief that one's own race is superior.*[2] **Sexism** is *prejudice, stereotyping, or discrimination, typically against women (and sometimes men), on the basis of sex.* Ethnic bias usually takes the form of denigrating a particular national or ethnic group, as in the case of Islamophobia, or the fear and hatred of Muslims. Prejudice and discrimination are both overt and subtle. Racial violence and obvious forms of sexual harassment or ethnic hatreds are apparent to most people; however, they can be so non-transparent as to

---

1   "Race and Ethnicity Defined," CliffsNotes, https://www.cliffsnotes.com/study-guides/sociology/race-and-ethnicity/race-and-ethnicity-defined.

2   Oxford Living Dictionaries, s.v. "racism," https://en.oxforddictionaries.com/definition/racism.

go unnoticed. Victims of such attitudes and actions are often keenly sensitive to any slights that might be interpreted as prejudice or discrimination.

Theories of Prejudice

There are a number of sociological theories used to explain prejudice.

Scapegoat theory refers to *the tendency to blame someone else for one's own problems, a process that often results in feelings of prejudice toward the person or group that one is blaming.* **Scapegoating** serves as *an opportunity to explain failure or misdeeds, while maintaining one's positive self-image.*[3]

A common form of scapegoating is marginalization. A person who for whatever reason does not conform to the values or norms of a group or organization may be singled out for ostracism and forced to take the blame for the failures or misdeeds of others. Conditions fraught with tension and ill feelings, as in the case of hostile cliques in a work situation, are environments where scapegoating often takes place, especially when there is a crisis or a bone of contention. On a larger scale, the scapegoating of Jews and others considered "undesirable" by the Nazis during the Third Reich in Germany (1933–1945) was a horrendous illustration of scapegoat theory.

After the Second World War, a noted psychologist, Theodor Adorno, developed a theory of personality to explain why groups and individuals foster, support, and condone wide-scale prejudice and discrimination against those who are marginalized within society. His **authoritarian personality theory** relates to *a state of mind or attitude characterized by belief in absolute obedience or submission to one's own authority, as well as the administration of that belief through the oppression of one's subordinates.*[4] Some of the characteristics of this theory apply to persons who hold conventional and rigid moral views of right and wrong. Other relevant traits relate to having a highly competitive nature, adhering to strict hierarchies, and not being well educated. Referring back to our description of prejudice, it is clear that someone with an authoritarian personality would by definition be prejudiced.

Culture theory *views prejudice as rooted in one's perception of cultural differences.* People who speak different languages, entertain uncommon beliefs, and have contrary values to the norm may be viewed in a negative light. Culture theory might offer another perspective on racism. While racism is often perceived as objections to one's skin color or other physical characteristics, prejudice against African-Americans may involve hostile attitudes directed towards their music tastes, hairstyles, spoken dialect, clothes, media stereotypes, and other characteristics that distinguish them from the dominant culture. Given that fear is often the by-product

---

3   "Scapegoat Theory," IResearchNet.com, https://psychology.iresearchnet.com/social-psychology/social-psychology-theories/scapegoat-theory/.

4   Richard West, *Introducing Communication Theory, Analysis and Application* (Content Technologies, Inc., 2016).

of distorted and oversimplified images of a social group, cultural differences can easily evoke prejudice.

Finally, **conflict theory** *views society as being in a perpetual state of conflict due to competition for limited resources.* It holds that the social order is maintained by domination and power, rather than consensus and conformity.[5] Implied by this theory is the idea that those in power believe it is in their interest is to "divide and rule," or generate a degree of conflict and confusion so as to keep the masses of people diverted, subordinate, and obedient. Karl Marx's idea of class conflict is a prime example of this theory.

Emory S. Bogardus sought to quantify prejudice by empirically measuring the degrees of closeness a dominant group enjoyed with members of diverse racial and ethnic groups. His scale was based on questions as to whether one would accept, on one hand, minority persons of various categories as a friend/family member, or conversely, at the other extreme as someone who should be barred from entering the country. Predictably, those groups who possessed similar cultural traits had a positive score on the social distance scale as opposed to those whose culture was considered foreign or objectionable. Groups publically maligned as hostile or dangerous, not surprisingly, would appear as less acceptable on this scale.

THEORIES OF DISCRIMINATION

Discrimination is often the by-product of prejudice. Sociologists tend to see discrimination as the result of a vicious cycle that may start with a mild form of prejudice, such as ethnocentrism, used to justify the superiority of one's own culture. Such attitudes directed towards a minority group may then cause that group to be socially disadvantaged, leading to various acts of discrimination that keep them in low-status situations. Consequently, discrimination would further lead to the widespread belief that a certain minority group is innately inferior, which stigmatizes them and reinforces the cycle of their subordination. While there are laws aimed at preventing discrimination in housing, employment, and other spheres of life, discrimination can be difficult to prove. Various seemingly believable reasons may be given for denying a minority person a job, for instance, even though the fundamental reason was objection to his or her race, ethnicity, religion, or gender. There is evidence that in a number of cities, African Americans find it more difficult to get a mortgage to buy a home, all of the factors being equal.

In terms of intergroup relations between a minority and the majority culture, there is a continuum ranging from acceptance to rejection. The most positive form of intergroup relations is **pluralism**, or *the encouragement of racial and ethnic acceptance on an*

---

5   "Conflict Theory," Investopedia, https://www.investopedia.com/terms/c/conflict-theory.asp.

equal basis. Moving down the line, there is **assimilation,** which is *where the dominant group over time absorbs the minority into its own culture.* With some notable exceptions, most immigrant ethnic groups have over several generations been assimilated into American society. Far less acceptable is **segregation,** or *the separation and subordination of a minority group from the dominant culture so as to minimize contact between the two groups.* The American system of apartheid, which legally segregated African Americans in a number of southern states for a hundred years, was a prime illustration of this sort of intergroup relations. **Internal colonization** and **population transfer,** which was the policy directed towards Native Americans during the nineteenth century, involved *herding of various tribes on to reservations* (population transfer), and *subjugating those populations into a condition of dependency* (internal colonization). The last, and by far the most inhumane pattern of majority/minority interaction is **genocide,** or *the elimination of an entire group of people through deliberate extermination.* Regrettably, over the past century there have been numerous genocides around the world. Whereas the United States has been moving in the direction of pluralism or multi-culturalism in recent years, its past history provides less desirous examples of tortured intergroup relations.

HISTORICAL DEMARCATIONS: RACE

Within the United States African Americans stand alone apart from other ethnic minorities because of their peculiar history. Prior to the formation of the American republic, African-Americans were transported to the new World as slaves. After the United States achieved its independence from Great Britain, slavery became institutionalized mostly in the southern states where there was a high demand for plantation labor to harvest a variety of crops, most particularly cotton. While **slavery** may take different forms, it is usually characterized as *the involuntary subjection of one person to another so as to become property that could be bought or sold and disposed of according to the wishes of a slave master.* In 1860, out of a total population of 31,183,562, there were 3,950,528 slaves in the United States, or 13% of the population.

After the Civil War, the former slave states enacted various laws known as the Jim Crow laws aimed at denying African Americans basic rights, including the right to vote, enjoyed by other American citizens. At the same time, social segregation was practiced throughout the United States. For the most part, African Americans accommodated themselves to the norms of segregation. Discrimination on a large scale against African Americans was reinforced by norms that only gradually began to be questioned.

After the Second World War, attitudes began to change. Major League Baseball was integrated in 1947 and demands to eliminate discriminatory laws and customs against African Americans became more vocal. In 1954, the US Supreme Court unanimously declared segregation in public schools to be unconstitutional, which accelerated actions aimed at promoting civil rights. Non-violent protests against Jim Crow laws eventually resulted in the Civil Rights Act of 1964 and the Voting Rights Act of 1965 outlawing discrimination and practices that inhibited voting behavior, giving African Americans full benefits of citizenship.

The fight to end discrimination in other parts of the county resulted in violent protests, resulting in laws used to incarcerate large numbers of black people. Although legal protections coupled with a greater degree of social acceptance has eliminated many of the barriers that divided races, the effects of racism are still prevalent in the United States today. According to the Henry J. Kaiser Fund, nearly a quarter of the African American population lived in poverty in 2018, nearly double the national average. A report compiled by the Economic Policy Institute found that African American unemployment is at least twice that of Whites based on 2018 figures. The death rate for Blacks from the COVID-19 virus shows a similar ratio. Other social statistics show that despite the changes that have taken place, many African Americans are still disadvantaged in the United States.

HISTORICAL DEMARCATIONS: ETHNICITY

The United States is a land of immigrants. Immigration has occurred through historical cycles. The first group of settlers to the United States came largely from the British Isles. From the mid-nineteenth century there was a wave of immigrants from Ireland and Germany. By far, the greatest wave occurred roughly between 1890 and 1920 with the arrival of a large number of the people from southern and eastern Europe. After the Second World War, and particularly after 1965 due to changes in the immigration laws, there has been a large influx of people from Asia, Africa, and Latin America. While the largest percentage of Americans are of European descent, the number of Latinos and immigrants from other parts of the world are growing at a faster rate. It is estimated that by the year 2050 white Americans of European descent will be a minority in the United States.

FIGURE 10.2. Immigrants Make America Great.

While many people coming to this country have sought opportunities for a better life, reasons for mass migration are more varied and complex. Disruptive conditions often prompted people to emigrate from their homeland. In recent years, refugees have fled to the United States due to unsettling or dangerous conditions in their country of origin. Drug and gang violence in Latin America, for instance, has forced many people to risk their lives in order to seek the promise of a safe haven in the United States. Such has been their desperation that millions have sought to enter the country illegally. A major social policy issue has been the legality of so-called DREAMERS, or children brought to the United States illegally, not of their own volition. Efforts to build a wall across the Southern border, separate immigrant children from their parents, and force those applying for legal residence in the United States to reside in Mexico to await the resolution of their case has created a major humanitarian crisis. With so much turmoil around the world, immigration pressures will continue to be of major importance in the years to come.

Even though the predominant myth is that Americans have opened their arms to people from around the world, the fact is that throughout its history there have been repeated efforts to exclude immigrants. Going back over a century, the passing of the 1882 Chinese Exclusion Act ended free immigration.

Through legal measures and diplomatic agreements, the government also found ways to exclude Japanese (and Koreans), Indians, and Filipinos. The national origins quota system enacted in 1924 narrowed the entryway for eastern and southern Europeans. Although territorial annexation and the need for Mexican labor for industrial and agricultural developments drove Mexican immigration to the United States since the late 19th century, deportation of Mexican workers prevented many Mexicans from attaining permanent residency in the United States.[6]

It was only after the Second World War that immigration has become more diverse. Today there remains a tension between those who from an ethnocentric perspective wish to limit immigration, and those who favor immigration so as to produce a multi-cultural society.

HISTORICAL DEMARCATIONS: GENDER

Dating back to the mid-nineteenth century, there has been a gradual evolution towards greater political, economic, and social rights for women. For centuries, women (like children) were considered dependents and therefore subordinate to husbands, fathers, and men in authority. The Seneca Falls Declaration in 1848 demanded "sovereignty for all free citizens," and provided the ideological platform for equal

---

6 Xiaojian Zhao, *Immigration to the United States after 1945* (Oxford University Press, 2016), http://americanhistory.oxfordre.com/view/10.1093/acrefore/9780199329175.001.0001/acrefore-9780199329175-e-72#.

rights between men and women. The Fourteenth amendment to the U. S. Constitution further proclaimed equality under the law. In 1875, Elizabeth Cady Stanton challenged the legality of women's subordinate position within marriage. Stanton, along with Susan B. Anthony, Carrie Chapman Catt, and others were instrumental in bringing about the Nineteenth Amendment in 1920 giving women the right to vote. Around the same time, Margaret Sanger founded the Birth Control League aimed at giving women access to birth control devices so as to establish control over reproduction.

FIGURE 10.3. Women's March in Los Angeles.

It was during the 1960s and 70s that the women's movement took a major step forward with the passage of an Equal Pay Act in 1963, the formation of the National Organization for Women in 1966, the enactment of Title IX of the Educational Amendments Act in 1972 prohibiting sex discrimination in schools, and the Roe v. Wade Supreme Court decision in 1973 which overturned state laws restricting abortion. More recently, attention has focused on combatting sexual harassment and violence towards women. In 1993, the Supreme Court ruled that sexual harassment in the workplace was illegal. Charges accusing men in high positions of using their power to sexually exploit women has challenged the culture of sexism that has long been prevalent. At the same time, sexual harassment can be so widely interpreted as to infringe upon one's personal freedom that is the foundation of an open society.

THEORETICAL MODELS OF GENDER

From the perspective of the three theoretical paradigms, first the **structural-functional** model defines gender in terms of complementary roles, or attitudes and activities a culture attributes to each sex. In other words, society is often seen to be most functional when men and women have clearly defined roles that do not necessarily overlap or conflict. As such, families in many societies are the most functional when there are two parents, each with a given set of roles. This might also apply to those societies which practice polygyny or the marriage of one person with multiple spouses. Implied also is the idea that there are certain jobs and activities for which men and women are best suited.

Looking at gender through the lens of the conflict perspective, the dominant concept is **gender stratification**, which involves *the unequal distribution of wealth and power based on gender*. From this perspective, traditional family patterns reinforce dynamics of inequality, which according to feminists, has perpetuated the subordination of women over the centuries, giving impetus to the struggle for women's rights. The legitimate application of the conflict paradigm to gender is not personal, i.e. attacking men (who have their own issues and concerns), but rather an assault against those institutional norms and values that perpetuate sexism.

The **interactionist model** approaches gender through the relations between men and women in everyday social situations. A theorist using this perspective would be interested in "sex talk," or the way men and women communicate together.

GENDER COMMUNICATION

Solid evidence and apocryphal observations have confirmed that men and women communicate differently. Apart from other considerations, there is ample evidence that men and women view the world through different lenses which often leads to conflicts and misunderstandings. Consequently, gender communication has engendered a number of theories that offer interesting perspectives of this topic.

The most notable theorist on gender communication, who has written widely on the subject, is Deborah Tannen. For men, according to Tannen, conversations are about negotiations. This is based an inner need to preserve their independence and avoid failure. Thus men use discourse competitively as a form of one-upmanship, often desiring to have the last word. Conversely, for women, conversation is about establishing a network of connections so as to preserve intimacy and avoid isolation. This mode of discourse is about seeking and giving confirmation and support. By the same token, Tannen makes a distinction between report and rapport talk. When asked how their day went, men tend to give a very brief report that may even consist of a single word. Women, on the other hand, when asked the same question, would fully elaborate, giving a full story of the day's events. Clearly, Tannen sees that gender communication is often miscommunication.

Sociologist Carol Gilligan, picking up on Lawrence Kohlberg's model of how children undergo moral development (Chapter Seven), examined how gender communication affected moral decision-making. She chose to concentrate on pre-teen juveniles who were old enough to understand moral issues but not yet ready to attach elaborate qualifications. Boys, she found, when confronted with a problem involving right and wrong, would tend to make a decisive moral judgment and treat it as a logical problem to be solved. Girls, on the other hand, viewed morality in less obvious and clear-cut terms and would often explore the problem by examining the various possibilities. It is not hard to see that Gilligan's findings bore a similar relation to those of Tannen.

The final theorist, Alga Khalsa Singh, looked at certain functional differences in male/female communication patterns. He believed that men tend to see the world in binary terms as either/or issues. An example of this is what he called "big man/little man" modes. When a male is in "big man" mode he is assertive and wants to be in control. "Little man" is the vulnerable boy who wants to be looked after. Singh claims that men vacillate between these two modes of being. Females, on the other hand, are natural multi-taskers who can do a number of things simultaneously without missing a beat. Unlike men, women gravitate between what Singh calls inner woman, meaning a person of deep feelings, and outer woman, or the person who demands recognition and respect. The problem for both men and women is to understand which mode is dominant at a particular time. Singh also believed that women are more self-correcting than men, or more likely to take responsibility for their words and actions.

Taken together, these theories suggest that even though men and women regularly communicate without much difficulty, there are gender-based approaches that often hampers discourse and interactions. On the other hand, one should be careful not to treat these differences as absolutes since people understand the world differently according to their level of consciousness.

As discussed in chapter eight, sociologist Deborah Tannen has argued that men tend to use *report talk*, which is conveying information in short direct phrases while women engage in *rapport talk*, which is an elaborate presentation of information often in the form of a narrative or story. Men and women also employ different forms of sex talk when they are in single sex groups as opposed to mixed sex groups.

Clearly, race, ethnicity, and gender provide major challenges to the unity and cohesion of American society, and in other societies as well. Given that we as a nation have become more polarized and distrustful of those who do not share similar thoughts, behaviors, and ideals, the challenge will be to transcend identity politics that often prevents people from achieving an inclusive consciousness of commonality.

STUDY QUESTIONS

1. Explain the perpetuation of racism in the United States in terms of Scapegoat Theory, Authoritarian Personality Theory, Culture Theory, and Conflict Theory.
2. Discuss the position of women in American society today from the perspective of the structural-functional, the conflict, and the interactionist paradigms. Which one of these models offers, in your opinion, the best explanation? Why or why not?
3. Drawing upon the theories of gender communication presented by Deborah Tannen, Carol Gilligan, and Alga Khalsa Singh, discuss a specific conversation you had with someone of the opposite sex.

Figure Credits

CHAPTER ELEVEN

Deviance and Social Control

WHAT IS DEVIANCE? In sociology, **deviance** describes *an action or behavior that violates social norms, including a formally enacted rule (e.g., crime), as well as informal violations of social norms (e.g., rejecting folkways and mores).* According to the literal interpretation of this definition, everyone is deviant since norm violation is a normal occurrence. Moreover, it is rare that someone doesn't violate a law, although for most people such infractions are relatively minor. The problem is further exasperated by the fact that norms are constantly changing. Decades ago wearing tattoos might have been considered deviant, but today they have become normative, especially among young people. Is deviance a state of being as well as an action? Mental illness may be considered deviant, but it is not an intentional action or behavior that violates social norms.

An important point is that deviance is predicated on motive, which is a reflection of consciousness. Deviance can sometimes be the result of drift, or attachment to a deviant group or mode of behavior in an attempt to satisfy some conscious or unconscious need or desire. On the other hand, calculated forms of deviance may result from a rational choice that is entered into after weighing various alternatives. This involves mental activity. While motive is essential in assessing the cause of behavior, the focus of sociology is concerned with explaining effects and consequences. At the same time, one cannot assess the effects without taking account of the causes.

SOCIAL FOUNDATIONS OF DEVIANCE

From a sociological perspective, there are certain general statements one can make about deviance. First of all, deviance varies according to cultural norms. As was mentioned earlier, deviance is norm violation, but norms vary from one culture to another. For instance, in certain Arab countries it would be deviant for women to go out in public without wearing a burqa, which is attire covering the whole body including the face, whereas in other Arab countries wearing just a hijab, or headscarf, would be normative. In western countries social nudity may be considered deviant or normative depending on the situation and cultural norms. This perspective relates to the structural-functional perspective.

Secondly, people become deviant when others define them that way. Someone may acquire a deviant reputation purely on the basis of being marginalized or disliked. In a social situation where there is much negative gossip, deviant behavior may be attributed to a person without any cause or reason. Social media has certainly contributed to this phenomenon, which can cause much harm. Since defining a person as deviant is an aspect of social interaction, this perspective pertains to the Interactionist model.

Finally, rule making and rule breaking involve power. It follows that people higher on the social ladder, who exercise more political power and authority, are more likely to evade responsibility for deviant actions than those having less power. This is because persons in authority have more resources and are better able to "cover their tracks" than those lacking such resources. For example, women who have been sexually abused by men in high positions have often, until recently, been afraid to speak out for fear of losing a job or suffering other negative consequences. Social inequality (conflict model) determines not only who suffers the most from deviance, but also how it is perceived within the wider society.

STRUCTURAL-FUNCTIONAL THEORIES OF DEVIANCE

The structural-functional model has spawned several theories that have attempted to explain why some people engage in deviant acts. One such theory, put forward by sociologist Robert Merton, is **strain theory**. This theory *explains deviance in terms of the association of means and goals.* Accordingly, Merton's typology consists of possible responses between one's desire for success and the means used to achieve this goal. What he called conformity refers to a legitimate means, such as hard work or the wise investment of financial resources, to achieve a legitimate goal like financial security. The other responses were innovation (legitimate goals but illegitimate means), ritualism (legitimate means to an illegitimate end), retreatism (negative means to a negative end), and rebellion or the seeking of new goals through new means. Merton believed that in American society the desire for material success outweighed the means for obtaining that success.

In critiquing strain theory, one might point out that material success is not a universal goal for many people and that success may be defined in many ways. Moreover, the means and goals are not always clearly defined, and people often vacillate between what they desire and what they hope to achieve.

From another perspective, Emile Durkheim put forward two explanations of why people become deviant. In what might be called **functional theory**, Durkheim argued that *far from being abnormal, crime and deviance are a natural part of society.* Even in a religious order, or some other organization devoted to high principles, there would always be some sort of deviance even if it was only a slight divergence from an accepted social pattern. Given that all societies possess rules, there is a need to regulate rule breakers, no matter how slight the offense. Additionally, it might be noted that some degree of deviance is necessary in order for any society to function properly.

Insofar as crime and deviance are natural, Durkheim further maintained that they reinforced social rules and values. For one thing, deviance and crime affirm cultural values. If there was no standard of right and wrong, how might one know the difference? Therefore, deviance provides a useful contrast to what a society holds to be positive or good or negative and wrong. Similarly, deviance clarifies moral boundaries. Using school or company property for one's own purpose may seem innocent and legitimate, but it might well violate an organizational norm. If such behavior existed on a massive scale, a formal rule would most likely be imposed with punitive consequences. Thus, deviance can help define the degree of what is or is not permissible. Another benefit of deviance is that it promotes social unity. Widespread crime in a given area may encourage residents to come together to form a neighborhood watch committee and so join in for a common cause. Finally, deviance encourages social change. The most notable example of this was prohibition that outlawed the production and sale of alcoholic beverages in the United States during the 1920s. The law was so widely ignored and violated that it was repealed in 1933.

INTERACTION THEORIES OF DEVIANCE

The most predominant theory related to the interactionist model is **labeling theory**. This theory posits that *deviance and conformity result from the responses of others.* Basically, labeling theory states that deviance is in the eye of the beholder, since it is based on perceptions rather than actions. There are two forms of labeling. **Primary deviance** involves *the initial violation of a norm or law.* **Secondary deviance** relates to *rule breaking that occurs in response to others.* In other words, a person who has been identified and isolated or ostracized by others may accept the deviant label as their own. For instance, people classified as thieves or "druggies" may associate with persons of those sub-cultures and thus identify themselves as such. *A deviant label that is so strong that it becomes part of a person's identity* is called a **stigma.** A convicted child sex offender who is listed on a register even after serving a prison sentence for this crime would be so stigmatized.

Labeling theory also pertains to whether or not one views an act as deviant. The possession and use of controlled substances in the United States is generally perceived as a crime, whereas in other countries, the Netherlands for instance, illegal drug use is seen as a medical issue. This phenomenon is referred to as the **medicalization of deviance.**

Similar to labeling theory is what sociologist Edwin Sutherland called **differential association theory**. It states that *people learn deviance through frequent association with significant others who engage in deviant acts.* The process of learning patterns of deviance and being regarded as such is at the heart of what interactionist theories are all about.

Another theory relevant to the Interactionist model is Neutralization theory, which was developed in 1957 by Gresham Sykes and David Matza. This theory, also known as Drift Theory, helps explain why delinquents drift in and out of delinquency. Accordingly, **neutralization and drift theory** proposes that *juveniles often vacillate between a sense of obligation to the law and activities deemed unlawful or deviant.* Drift presupposes that delinquents tend to move back and forth between normative and delinquent behaviors. As such, "justified theft" would explain the case of an employee that sees his or her wages cut so they can then justify stealing from their employer because they are earning less money than before. Essentially, the employee feels they 'deserve' it. According to Sykes and Matza, most delinquents have conventional values, beliefs and attitudes as those" of the rest of normative society. "Some juveniles, however, learn techniques that allow them to "neutralize" such values and attitudes temporarily." Such a theory allows delinquents to temporarily abandon social mores and thus neutralize the hold of society on the individual.[1]

CONFLICT THEORIES OF DEVIANCE

All theories related to the conflict paradigm follow the same line of reasoning. Assuming that inequality is based on the distribution of power in society, it follows that those on the lower end of the scale are the most powerless. By contrast, the wealthier classes who make the rules and possess most of the resources can resist the consequences of their deviance. Therefore, the burden of guilt and punishment falls heaviest upon the poor.

Deviance is also associated with capitalism. Starting with the premise that capitalism is a system of private ownership that generates social inequality, it follows that inequality results from competition for scarce resources, which is central to a system of private ownership. Competition encourages both innovation and corruption as a means of getting ahead and achieving success. Therefore, capitalism by encouraging corruption is instrumental in encouraging deviance.

---

1   Seth McDonald, "Neutralization and Drift Theory: An Overview," Wikia, http://criminology.wikia.com/wiki/Neutralization_and_Drift_Theory:_an_overview.

Thus stated, theories derived from the conflict paradigm tend to flip the coin by suggesting that most crime is **white-collar crime**, or *crimes committed by the more affluent classes in the course of their work*. Such crimes fall into two categories. **Occupational crimes** involve *offenses committed in the workplace by individuals seeking their own self-interest*, whereas **corporate crimes** are those *offenses committed by corporate executives for the purpose of benefitting themselves and their companies*. Occupational crimes are numerous and include fraud (stealing), embezzlement and bribery, and swindles (scams). The fastest growing body of crime in recent years has involved cybercrime, which reaches into many spheres of life. The ability of hackers to retrieve personal data from

FIGURE 11.1. Policeman Handcuffing a Teenager.

computers puts people's financial information at risk and is a major social problem. Corporate crime can take many forms from **organized crime**, which is *a business that provides illegal goods and services* to efforts by corporations to buy political influence (bribery). One of many examples involved a defense contractor named Brent R. Wilkins who in 2006 received nearly $100 million in government work in exchange for giving more than $600,000 to congressional campaigns.

THE CRIMINAL JUSTICE SYSTEM

The **criminal justice system** includes the police who are charged with enforcing the law, the courts which determine whether a person is innocent or guilty, and the correctional system that punishes those convicted of a crime. In the United States there are various levels of police which have jurisdiction over local, county, state, and federal regions. Apart from the Federal Bureau of Investigation (FBI), certain government agencies have their own policing powers, such as the US Immigration and Customs Enforcement (or ICE) which is under the jurisdiction of the Department of Homeland Security (DHS). Clearly, the United States is not an under-policed society.

The killing and harassment of Black suspects, often by White policemen, has brought to the fore the problem of police brutality and discrimination, which has long been a concern within communities of color. The murder of George Floyd by a White policeman in June 2020 set off days of protest sparked by the "Black Lives Matter" movement and the call for significant police reform.

There are different levels of courts as well that adjudicate cases with their various jurisdictions according to relevant laws. The vast majority of criminal cases are subject to state laws, which of course may vary from state to state. Federal courts deal with cases under federal law, such as the violation of one's civil rights. Sometimes there are conflicts. For example, certain states have

FIGURE 11.2. Alfred P. Murrah Federal Building in the aftermath of the 1995 Oklahoma City Bombing.

passed laws legalizing marijuana. However, the use of this drug is forbidden under federal law. The matter is then left to Congress or the courts to decide.

The correctional system involves both non-custodial and custodial forms of punishment. Non-custodial sentences include probation or community service and are often reserved for those convicted of lesser offenses and in some cases first-time offenders. Custodial or prison sentences are for more serious crimes, particularly violent crimes. It is an anomaly in the United States that while violent crime has declined since the 1990s, the incarceration rate has steadily increased from the 1970s. Overall, the United States by far leads other countries in the rates of persons locked up for various crimes. The United States is also one of a handful of countries including China, Saudi Arabia, Iran, and North Korea that engage in capital punishment.

There is also a racial bias with regards to arrests, convictions, and incarceration. According to the Sentencing Project's *Annual Report for 2019*, the incarnation rate for Black Americans was 1,408 per 100,000 population compared to 275 per 100,000 for White Americans and 378 per 100,000 for Hispanic Americans. The rates for women are much lower but there is a rough correspondence. The criminal justice system remains one of the best indicators of the degree of racism in the United States.

In summation, crime as a global phenomenon is linked to the dynamics of culture. In smaller close-knit societies with a strong normative structure, the

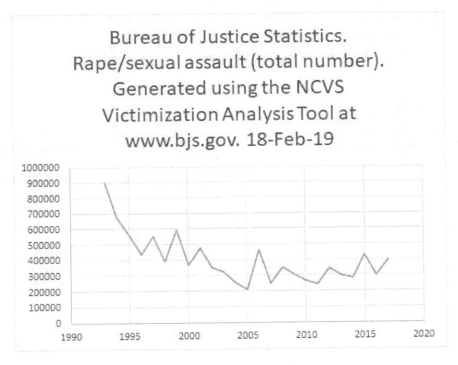

FIGURE 11.3. Bureau of Justice Rape & Sexual Assault Statistics.

amount of crime and deviance is far less than in large heterogeneous societies where there are many laws and weaker norms. For instance, the United States has seven times the amount of violent crime and twice the amount of total crime as does Denmark. Crime rates are also affected by the collective consciousness of a society. Americans pride themselves on their individualism. Individualism can generate a sense of separation that generates fear. People in the United States have a greater fear of crime and concerns about personal safety than indicated by the actual amount of crime. There is a clear correlation between the fear of crime and gun ownership. Data compiled by the Congressional Research Service shows that Americans possess 48% of the 650 million civilian-owned guns in the world. The connection between the availability of guns and violent crime should be obvious. While crime is universal and natural, it reflects the character of a given society, which can raise many interesting questions.

STUDY QUESTIONS

1. How might a conflict theorist explain the difference between why a white middle class businessman and a poor black man, convicted of the same crime would likely receive different sentences?
2. Give contrasting arguments as to whether illicit drug use should be considered a medical problem or treated as criminal activity.
3. Discuss the ways that crime and deviance may be functional within a society.

Figure Credits

CHAPTER TWELVE

Sexuality & Society

THE QUESTION, *WHAT is sex?* may seem obvious, but is it? Sex as a force of nature is both complex and pervasive throughout the natural world. As an archetype, sex represents polarity or the relation between positive (male) and negative (female) energies. Depictions of this appear in the Chinese yin/yang symbolism showing the female (yin) and the male (yang) duality that governs all phenomenal relationships. This aside, sex is a matter of consciousness which is why it is such a dominant factor in people's lives. People spend far more time thinking and desiring sex than engaging in the physical act. Because sex is a preoccupation on the three planes (mental, emotional, and physical) of one's being, it often invokes other reactions that may be harmful or beneficial. Sexual desire can lead to violence if there is a mean or aggressive intent. Likewise, sex can be the culmination of intimacy or emotional love, which are positive attractive forces. Sexuality has social consequences which is why it is important to the study of sociology.

What does the phrase "to make love" mean? The most frequent answer would be to have sex, but if we examine this statement closely the literal interpretation would be that love corresponds to sex. Is this true? Clearly, people recognize that love has a far greater meaning and that sex is merely an expression of only a certain aspect of love, if indeed it expresses love at all.

So, what is love? There are multiple definitions. It may refer to a warm personal attachment or deep affection between two or more people. Moreover, it may suggest a close friendship as indicated by the Greek word *philos*. The term *agape* relates to charity, altruistic, or spiritual love, such as the love for humankind. Finally, *Eros* as an expression of love pertains to desire or sexual attraction, which is preliminary to coitus or the physical act of sex. Ultimately, love is an expression of the soul, meaning connectedness or the sense of non-separateness.

Biologically speaking, males and females are differentiated on the basis of **primary sex characteristics**, which *relate to male and female reproductive organs,* and **secondary sex characteristics** that pertain to *other physical traits such as* *body shape, breasts, facial hair, voice pitch, among other things that distinguish males from females.* Sex also refers to social rules and expectations (norms) that are relevant to each gender along with standards of behavior (values) that are culturally defined. Sociologists apply the term **sexual scripts** to *shared beliefs concerning what a society defines as appropriate behavior for each sex.* These scripts vary in a latitudinal way across different societies and cultures, as well as historically in a longitudinal manner over time. Factors that have conditioned changes in sexual norms and values include contraceptive techniques, the influence of mass media, and the decline of rigid moral rules. Over the past half-century or so, the growth of the modern women's rights movement and the de-mystification of sex brought on by a greater degree of social intercourse and familiarity between males and females has influenced patterns of sexual behavior.

THEORETICAL ANALYSIS OF SEXUALITY

The structural-functional approach to sex relates to how social institutions work to make sexual activity functional. First and foremost, all societies require some form of sexual regulation. Folkways that occur in all societies are referred to as cultural universals. A cultural universal is the **incest taboo,** which is *any cultural rule or norm that prohibits sexual relations between closely related persons.*[1] There are various reasons for this restriction, but one factor of importance is that it forces members of a family or a small, blood-related group to have a wider sphere of sexual activity so as to expand social contacts and thus contribute to the health of the race. Marriage is another effective way of controlling sexual behavior. This said, the rate of adultery in the United States has been on the increase over the past few decades. While accurate figures are hard to come by, the best estimates suggest that twenty-two percent of married men and fourteen percent of married women have had extramarital affairs. Another form of sexual regulation is courtship norms. These rules vary considerably around the world. In Iran, dating is tightly controlled by families. There are parts of Africa that practice arranged marriages which severely restrict dating, if it exists at all. In the Far East, particularly Japan and Korea, boys and girls generally do not go out together before college. Such a lack of opportunities places limits on sexual activity. Furthermore, all major religions reinforce norms that control sexual behavior. As societies become more secular and diverse, restrictions on sex tend to become weaker.

From a structural-functional standpoint, defined sexual and relationship roles are conducive to social stability. Over the centuries, it has been the duty of men to protect women (and children) and it is a particularly strong norm in more traditional societies. By the same token, men have been viewed as providers whose role is to take care of family members. Likewise, the care and upbringing of children has usually been the

---

1   Serena Nanda, *Cultural Anthropology* (Content Technologies, 2017).

function of women. As women have assumed a greater economic presence in society, they have demanded equal rights in the workplace and at home. Consequently, these more gender-specific roles have become less pronounced, although in many cases those expectations still remain. In parts of the world that retain a hierarchical social structure, rigid sex and gender roles are still dominant.

Sexual norms from a conflict perspective reflect cultural patterns of social inequality. Feminists have tended to adopt this perspective. The emphasis on male dominance is linked to customary patterns of interaction that focus on the double-standard, or norms allowing males greater sexual freedom than females. Likewise, the tendency to give males greater recognition in a variety of social situations has reinforced the tilt towards gender inequality. An obvious example of this inequality is pay differentials given to men and women, often for doing the same job. The issue of rape and date rape, which is as much a violent crime as a sexual crime, is directly tied in with (usually) male sexual aggression. According to the Rape & Incest National Network (RAINN),[2] there are on average 321,500 victims of rape and sexual assault above the age of twelve in the United States each year. About ninety percent of rape victims are female. There is also a high percentage of rapes in confined environments such as prisons and the military. Some statistics imply that nearly a quarter of undergraduate women experience acts of rape or sexual assault during their college years.

The ongoing debate over abortion and reproductive rights is essentially about the control of women's sexuality. The right to life issue versus reproductive choice is as much about politics and it is about morality, and is a bone of contention between governmental agencies, religious organizations, and a host of interest groups. This debate is one of a number of issues that separate social conservatives from those with a more liberal perspective.

Sexual violence against women in particular has some relation to the treatment of women as sexual objects. The so-called "playboy syndrome" which portrays women as objects of sexual pleasure for men is one example. The primary culprit, however, would appear to be advertising. Advertisers have long realized that sexual arousal can be used to sell products if the items for sale can be made to appear "sexy." The deluge of provocative adverts is about stimulating one's acquisitive desires to buy goods and services and to make purchasing choices, but impacts the entire culture.

Inequality also relates to those groups whose sexual orientation has marginalized them from mainstream society. This was more of an issue in the past when sexual practices, like homosexuality, were severely censured and in some cases criminalized. The legal and social acceptance in recent decades of those whose sexual preference was considered outside the norm has revealed a greater tolerance for all forms of sexual expression.

---

2 "Victims of Sexual Violence: Statistics," Rainn, https://www.rainn.org/statistics/victims-sexual-violence.

SEXUAL ORIENTATION

Sexual orientation pertains to *a person's sexual identity in relation to the gender to which they are attracted—the fact of being heterosexual, homosexual, or bisexual.* By far the most common, and some would say the most natural form of sexual orientation, is **heterosexuality**, which is *the sexual attraction of a male to a female and is the basis for propagating the species.* **Homosexuality** involves *same sex relations.* **Bisexuality** concerns *sexual attraction and relations with members of both sexes.* **Asexuality** is *the lack of sexual attraction to others, or low or absent interest in or desire for sexual activity and may be considered the lack of a sexual orientation.* A final sexual inclination is **transgender**, which is *denoting or relating to a person whose sense of personal identity and gender does not correspond with their birth sex.*[3] Masturbation is a common practice for males and females as a way to sublimate sexual desire.

The question of what gives us a specific sexual orientation is largely speculative. Some would argue that sexual identity is learned behavior derived from social interaction. It would follow that certain experiences, cultural proclivities, and social expectations influence one's sexual interests. On the other hand, others would contend that sexual orientation is an innate facet of our being. From the perspective of reincarnation by which one carries over certain tendencies from one life to the next, homosexuality and transgender could be explained in terms of living many concurrent lives as one sex and then being born as a person of the opposite sex. Thus, such a person might feel themselves to be a man or a woman even though they are not that particular sex. In this context, sexual orientation is more a psychological issue rather than a biological or sociological matter.

FIGURE 12.1. Gay Couple with Child at San Francisco Parade.

---

3 Oxford Living Dictionaries, s.v. "transgender," https://en.oxforddictionaries.com/definition/transgender.

SEXUAL CONTROVERSIES

Since sexuality is such a potent and pervasive force, it is the focus of a number of controversies and issues that affect the wider society. While it is commonly rumored that prostitution is the world's oldest profession, evidence of the sex trade can be found at least as far back as the ancient world. **Prostitution** is defined as *the practice or occupation of engaging in sexual activity with someone for payment.*[4] The number of prostitutes is staggering. Estimates suggest that tens of millions of women around the world are prostitutes at any given time either voluntarily or through forced sex slavery.[5] The number of female prostitutes in the United States could be around one million.

The social value of prostitution is debatable. From the structural-functional perspective, prostitution may offer an acceptable outlet for sexual energies. It is also a business that provides a service based on free-market principles. Seen from the conflict model, prostitution is a highly exploitative enterprise that preys on women and children, forcing many into a virtual condition of slavery. Many prostitutes were sexually abused before the age of eighteen and for some, sexual commerce is a means to acquire drugs to feed an addiction. While numerous countries and most states within the United States have laws aimed at outlawing the sex trade, such efforts, considering its pervasiveness, are often ineffectual. The pervasiveness of information technologies has changed the face of prostitution by allowing sex workers to deal directly with prospective clients, thus avoiding the middleman (pimps).

A somewhat related issue is pornography. Defined as such, **pornography** includes *printed or visual material containing the explicit description or display of sexual organs or activity, intended to stimulate erotic rather than aesthetic or emotional feelings.*[6] Figures vary widely as to the extent of pornography. Suffice it to say, that it is a multi-billion-dollar industry that covers the sale of magazines, videos, e-mails, and on-line merchandise. The worst feature of the pornographic industry is the pervasiveness of child pornography. According to the US Department of Justice,[7] nearly 300,000 children are in danger of falling victim to sex exploitation. The possession of child pornography in the United States is considered to be a serious felony that could put one in prison for many years.

---

4   Oxford Living Dictionaries, s.v. "prostitution," https://en.oxforddictionaries.com/definition/prostitution.

5   Prostitution, "Extent of Women's Prostitution." https://sites.google.com/site/prostitution1/definitions-of-prostitution/extent-of-women-s-prostitution.

6   "Pornography," University of Iowa, Student Legal Services, 2018, https://legal.studentlife.uiowa.edu/protect-your-future/pornography/.

7   US Department of Justice. "Facts and Statistics," https://www.nsopw.gov/en-US/Education/factsstatistics.

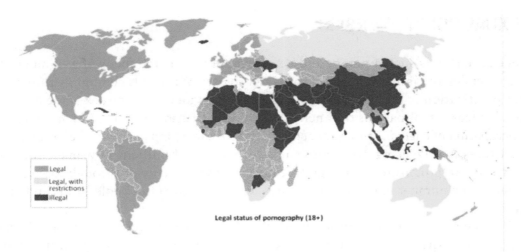

Legal

Legal, with restrictions

illegal

Legal status of pornography (18+)

FIGURE 12.2. Pornography Law Map.

In a society awash with sexual messages that touch all age groups, it is not surprising that many adolescents are sexually active. Close to half of American teenagers reportedly have had sex. The frequency of adolescent sexual activity has consequently led to the issue of teenage pregnancies. According to data from the Centers for Disease Control,[8] the teen birth rate in the United States reached a high point in the 1960s and has fallen steadily ever since, save the period from the mid-1980s and 90s, when the rate leveled off and even increased slightly. By comparison, the United States has one of the highest rates of teen births among western developed countries. The relative decline in the rate of teenage births may be attributable to better sex education and the availability of contraceptive devices. The vast majority of teen births occur out of wedlock, which corresponds to a decline in the marriage rate. The impact of provocative mass advertising and sexually charged media on teen pregnancies would appear to have some correlation.

In terms of the structural-functional paradigm, teen pregnancy may be functional or not, depending on the culture. In societies where couples marry at a young age and enjoy a large support network, pregnancy and childbirth among adolescents may be encouraged and considered normative. This is not the case in more developed countries. From a conflict perspective, teen pregnancy and childbirth is reflective of race, ethnicity, and social class. In terms of race and ethnicity, African Americans, Latinos, and Native Americans have a higher percentage of out-of-wedlock pregnancies than do whites and Asian Americans. This disparity reflects class differences, which fall more heavily on lower-class minority teens.

---

8   "Teen Births," Center for Disease Control, https://www.cdc.gov/nchs/fastats/teen-births.html.

Passion, desire, and the proclivity for sex varies considerably from person to person and is part of an individual's sphere of consciousness and psychological makeup. At the same time, the expression of sex is modified by a society's norms and values. The preoccupation with sex is subject to the ebb and flow of historical cycles. The objectification of sexual knowledge and practice has confronted pre-existing cultural restraints with unprecedented complexities and difficulties. How societies cope with the issues surrounding sex will pose challenges for the future.

STUDY QUESTIONS

1. Which paradigm (structural-functional or conflict) best explains the relationships of men and women with respect to sexuality today? Give reasons and examples.
2. From a structural-functional perspective, discuss how prostitution and pornography might be considered both functional and dysfunctional.
3. What impact has social media had on sexual behavior? Has it encouraged or limited sexual activity? Explain.

Figure Credits
Fig. 12.1: Copyright © by Caitlin Childs (CC BY-SA 2.0) at https://commons.wikimedia.org/wiki/File:Gay_couple_with_child_at_San_Francisco_Gay_Pride.jpg.
Fig. 12.2: Source: https://commons.wikimedia.org/wiki/File:Pornography_law_map.png.

Foundational Institutions

THE PILLARS OF all societies are institutions. Basically, all institutions can be placed within six distinctive categories. The first and foremost institution is the family, which performs at the microlevel all the functions of other institutions. Families are an essential element of social cohesion that adapts and changes within the life experiences of its members and through pressures and influences within the society itself. No society can function without some sort of government that is part of the political process. Politics is about the exercise of power and authority at various levels. Economics has to do with the production, distribution and consumption of goods and services, facilitated by exchange systems primarily in the form of money. Economic institutions are perhaps the major factor leading to globalization. The cultural foundation of all societies is religion and spirituality. Religion is the structural basis of spirituality, whereas spirituality is the essence of soul life that is experiences individually and collectively. Both a modifier and reflection of consciousness is education. More than just the accumulation of knowledge, education is about the development of the mind (thinking processes) and expanding one's sphere of awareness. It is also a determining factor as to the application of one's skills and abilities and future job status. Health and medicine refers to the maintenance of one's well-being on all levels. This is carried out through the scientific process of determining the causes of an illness and prescribing a proper remedy. It is also a metaphor for the degree of stability and functionality within a society.

CHAPTER THIRTEEN

The Family

THE NEXT SIX chapters will be devoted to a more detailed discussion of basic social institutions. You will recall that institutions are enduring and complex social structures that shape our lives. As such, institutions are the foundation and scaffolding of any society. The family is considered to be a primary institution since it performs the duties in microcosm of other institutions. For instance, the family has a political role since it lays down rules for its members and exercises a degree of authority. Economically, families need to earn money, pay taxes and bills, and maintain, officially or unofficially, a budget. Families are agents of socialization (education), they impart core values and beliefs (religion), and they are the first line of defense for maintaining health and well-being.

While I am sure that many of you think of family primarily in terms of your parents and siblings, it has a wider meaning and application. Apart from those who share a common ancestry, the notion of a family can be broadly applied, ranging from people who live together in a single dwelling to a crime organization, such as the Mafia.

Furthermore, family can be understood in terms of consciousness and identity. People who feel an affinity for what they might call their "soul group," sometimes say "We are just like family," referring to a connection of intimacy. As such, family may be applied loosely as a focus of identity to those of a particular subculture, race or ethnicity. Broadly speaking, from a more inclusive consciousness, one may think of the human family as a single group. Underscoring each of these applications is the idea of connection, whether it is close and intimate or distant and seemingly remote. Hence, family conceptually is closely tied to our understanding of society.

FAMILY DISTINCTIONS

In a sociological sense, the **Family** is *a social institution that unites people into cooperative groups.* Since there are various kinds of groups that fall under the heading of family, it is important to make certain differentiations. One kind of family is a household. A **household** *is composed of one or more people who occupy a housing unit.* Taking the definition of family from the US Census Bureau, households consist of two or more individuals who are related by birth, marriage, or adoption, although they may also include other unrelated people such as lodgers or tenants.[1]

A **clan** refers to *a group of close-knit and interrelated families.* In a clan, people claim descent from a common ancestor. A tribe is one of the earliest forms of social organizations uniting those that have a close or distant biological connection. Developmentally or historically, a **tribe** is *a social group existing outside of or before the development of states.* Furthermore, it is a group of distinct people dependent on land for their livelihood who are largely self-sufficient and not integrated into the national society.[2] The strong bonds of consciousness that unite a clan or tribe suggest that persons in such groups may have been joined together over previous lifetimes. In the modern world, tribalism exists in the form of ethnic, religious, or racial attachments, and is often a primary source of conflict and discord within nation-states.

Family connections in various degrees are included in the idea of **kinship**. This term is used by anthropologists as a method for studying *mainly small traditional societies based upon gender, age, and family ties.* Kinship groups may be defined in terms of size. A **nuclear family** is *a small-sized family unit comprising parents and biological and adoptive offspring.* Single-parent families are also considered within the category of nuclear families. An **extended family** consists of *a nuclear family plus a wider circle of kin such as uncles, aunts, grandparents, and cousins.* A distinctive characteristic of an extended family is that all members of this kinship group live together or reside in close proximity to one another.

Central to family formation and development is **marriage**, defined as *a legal relationship usually involving sexual activity, economic cooperation, and child bearing.* Although marriage is a contractual arrangement most often conducted through some sort of ritual, there has been a growing trend for couples to live together outside of marriage, so defined. This is particularly true in the United States where according to the US Census Bureau[3] there were 8.5 million opposite-sex couples in 2018 co-habiting together. Also, there is an increasing number of same sex marriages, which has further widened the more traditional understanding of marriage as the bringing together of both sexes in wedlock.

Over much of the world, the legal form of marriage is **monogamy** or *the joining together of two people, usually a man and a woman.* In roughly a third of the world,

---

1   United States Census Bureau. "Programs and Surveys," https://www.census.gov/programs-surveys/cps/technical.../subject-definitions.html.

2   "History," Tribal News Service of India, https://tribalnewsindia.com/?page_id=1553.

3   US Census Bureau. "America's Families and Living Arrangements: 2011, Table UC1," https://www.census.gov/population/www/socdemo/hh-fam/cps2011.html.

FIGURE 13.1. Bengali Marriage.

polygamy is allowed, which is *the uniting of a single person with multiple spouses.* In most cases this involves a man having more than one wife, the permitted number usually determined by custom. There are a few examples of **polyandry** in which *a wife is married to more than one husband.* A **family of orientation** is *the family one is born into and raised in.* A **family of procreation** is *the family that one creates by producing offspring.*

Families are also delineated by residence and lines of authority. In the United States and other western societies, it is *the common practice for couples to set up households on their own.* This is referred to as a **nonlocal residence pattern.** In more traditional societies, where married couples live within the boundaries of an extended family, the residence pattern is **patrilocal** *if one lives with the husband's family*, and **matrilocal,** *if it is with the wife's family.* Similarly, *if authority within a family is exercised by the male head, whether a husband/father or some elder*, it constitutes a **patriarchal system.** A **matriarchal system** exists when *the oldest females (grandmothers) control the* *economic and cultural life of a society.* Certain Native American tribes are said to have been organized this way. The same could be said for single-parent families under the authority of the mother. In modern secular societies, the tendency has been towards an egalitarian system in which authority and resources are shared.

THEORETICAL APPROACHES TO THE FAMILY

The structural-functional model "sees the family as a social institution that performs certain essential tasks. If these functions are not carried out, then the family is said to be dysfunctional." Society can be compared to the human body that has different parts that have a different role to play. "The family is the backbone of the society and if it fails to pass on certain values" and norms to its members then the social order weakens and suffers.[4] One characteristic of the American family structure which differentiates it from certain Asian cultures is the relative lack of respect shown to the elderly. Consequently, this often weakens family cohesiveness.

The structural-functional approach further mandates that families perform four main functions, namely sex and procreation, physical and emotional security, socialization, and social placement. Sex and procreation are obvious family functions, however approximately forty percent of the children born in the United States are born out of wedlock, which some see as a serious threat to family stability. Healthy families provide stability and security for its members, especially children. Socialization includes rules for safety, as well as providing the basis for social and cultural learning. Social placement for younger family members is predicated on ascription, which is the status held by one's parents.

Seen from the conflict perspective, families mirror the degree of inequality in any society. Wealth or poverty is closely tied to how resources are allocated and transferred. More than one in five children in the United States live in poverty whereas two in five children reside in low-income families. The so-called "economic despair" model shows that as the gap between the bottom and mid-income distribution of wealth widens, middle-class standards of living become increasingly out of reach for economically disadvantaged youths.

Inheritance also plays an important role in furthering inequality. Fortunes are often made through the conveyance of wealth and property that has been acquired over generations. According to *Forbes Magazine*, among the richest four hundred billionaires in the United States, thirty to forty percent obtained their wealth through inheritances. While economic opportunities do exist, the notion that the United States is purely a meritorious society remains largely a myth.

---

4   Tamara Small-Kerr, "Structural Functionalism Theory," July 15, 2012, http://structuralfunction alismtheory.blogspot.com/2012/07/structural-functionalism-theory_15.html.

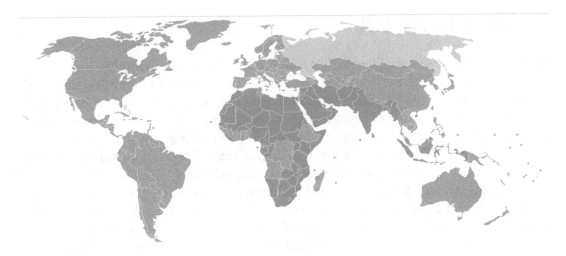

FIGURE 13.2. Polygamy World Map—Green Shows Countries That Allow Polygamy.

Within the family structure, patriarchy and matriarchy reinforce inequality based on gender. Since families mirror trends in the wider society, hierarchical patterns in families will mirror those in other institutions. For instance, the CEOs of large corporations are overwhelmingly male. As men and women become more conscious of their individual needs and identities, and as gender roles become less well-defined, gender-based hierarchies tend not to be so exclusive and rigid.

The interactionist view of family is based on shared and conflicting perspectives among family members. Not all persons see family life the same way. Husband/fathers, wife/mothers, and children often have different perceptions of how persons in the family interact with one another, and the degree to which the family is functional or dysfunctional. In many cases, these perceptions do not square with the facts. Teenagers often feel that their parents hate them when the opposite is usually the case. A stay-at-home wife/mother, who is tasked with household chores plus the care and management of children, may have a less-than-enthusiastic view of the family than a husband/father whose role as the primary provider may excuse him from tedious family chores. Perceptions of the family are linked to changes in social status. The breadwinner has customarily held an important status, which may be diminished if he or she becomes unemployed. Separation or divorce often creates confusion for children in terms of changing statuses, lines of authority, and loyalties. Perceptions by family members are subject to change over the course of the life cycle. What makes the family so complex (and interesting) is that it is continually shaping its members perceptual reality in ways that are often unpredictable.

STAGES OF FAMILY LIFE

Families, like individuals, pass through various stages of life. The cycle begins with mate selection of which there are two kinds. The one which you are most familiar with involves free choice. Males and females are generally free to select a potential mate based on any of a number of characteristics they deem important. A person's values and expectations often play a big role in selecting with whom to establish an enduring relationship. Factors involved in free choice mate selection include attraction/compatibility; social characteristics such as race, ethnicity, religion, and class; and also propinquity, which is proximity or the state of being close to someone.

Another form of mate selection is **arranged marriage,** which is *a type of marital union where the bride and groom are selected by their families.* Depending upon the culture, a person may have some degree of latitude in choosing a prospective spouse, but parents or elders have the final word. In some instances, a professional matchmaker may be used. The reasons for arranged marriages relate to dowry or property transfers, social status, and continuous arrangements, such as joining together of extended family members beyond the incest taboo.

The second stage is creation of the institution of marriage. There is much glamour and romance surrounding marriage that is fed by a vast media culture. Couples are often lured into this ideal marriage by films, books, and magazine articles that purport to show marital bliss, leading to a life of mutual happiness and fulfilment. More often than not, couples are faced with the realities of marriage, which include all the duties, practicalities, and responsibilities of maintaining the institution. In this sense, marriage becomes a partnership in conjunction with other functions, such as child rearing.

The next stage of family life is parenting. There are four styles of parenting. The **authoritarian** style is where *parents exercise total authority over their children, who have little freewill of their own.* Adjunct to this style is **hyperparenting**, which is *when a parent over-indulges, controls, or encourages perpetual interaction with a child that limits independence, creates insecurity, and stifles creativity.* **Authoritative** parenting *allows the child some degree of negotiating rights and decision-making within a structure of rules and responsibilities.* **Permissive** parenting is generally *a very relaxed style in which boundaries are unclear, the rules are intermitted, and when applied are often inconsistent.* Finally, the **uninvolved** mode of childrearing refers to *a parent who is not around or is not engaged in the responsibilities of parenting.* This characterizes the dysfunctional family where the parent may fall victim to drug and alcohol abuse, or where children are abandoned and to a large extent, forced to fend for themselves. The nearly half-million children in foster care in the United States are an indication of this problem.

Family rules fall into four categories. Moral rules essentially establish values of right and wrong. Safety rules are designed to protect the child against possible dangers, such as playing with fire or running into a street without proper caution. Civility rules are proper manners and the various folkways that condition amicable relationships. Children usually do not have a problem with these kinds of rules; however, personal rules that affect a child's activities and behavior patterns which they consider their own prerogative are often a bone of contention. As a child matures, personal rules become more explicit and important.

The final stage of family life concerns the later years. After children have grown up and left home, parents have to adjust to the "empty nest syndrome." Couples often assume the role of grandparents, which is affected by the proximity to their children's families. Retirement can bring greater freedom but also uncertainty and an adjustment to new statuses. Furthermore, issues of health and financial security come into play. The separation of generations in countries like the United States often creates anxieties and hardships for older people. Elderly people sometimes gravitate to retirement communities looking to associate with those having common interests and circumstances.

TRANSITIONS AND PROBLEMS OF FAMILIES IN THE UNITED STATES

The family in the United States is experiencing a number of pressures and challenges that are changing its structure and functions. Although the divorce rate has been on the increase for over a century, it has climbed to new heights particularly between the 1970s and the 1990s. The divorce rate closely parallels the rate of marriage. As the number of marriages dipped from the 1990s, so have the number of divorces. Likewise, the age of marriage for both males and females has risen dramatically since the 1950s. Delaying marriage has caused a drop in the number of marriages and consequently the number of divorces. The reasons for the overall climb of divorce over the past forty years are varied; some are personal and others sociological. One major factor has been a change in the status and role of women in the United States, which has undermined to some degree traditional family hierarchies. There are many other causes as well, not the least of which are changes in consciousness expressed through a desire for greater personal independence and self-expression.

Another significant challenge has been the decline of two-parent families. According to the Pew Research Center, between 1960 and 2014 the number of two-parent families that were never divorced fell from 73% to 46%. Over the same period, the number of single-parent families rose from 9% to 26%. Seven percent of all families in 2014 included cohabiting parents. This dramatic shift in family structure has had widespread social consequences affecting the poverty rate, especially for women, among other things. The rate for African Americans is significantly higher than for

FIGURE 13.3. Surrogate Parents Attending Birth.

whites. Roughly 85% of single-parent families are headed by women. The full impact of this trend is woven into numerous social patterns.

Another trend has been a slight rise in the number of gay, lesbian, bisexual, and transgender families (LGBT). According to a New York Times article, based on tax returns for same sex couples in 2014, there were 183,280 gay and lesbian marriages in the United States, roughly a third of one percent of all marriages. Figures indicate that the number of gay, lesbian, and transgender people is far less that what most Americans perceive it to be. Based on 2010 data, there were about 646,000 homosexual households.

Divorce and the decline of the two-parent family raise serious questions as to the fate of the institution of family itself. Some would argue that the break-up of families has caused great social harm and that efforts should be directed towards reinforcing the solidarity of the traditional family. Others maintain that the family is going through a phase of transition and will become solidified in some functional form. As previously stated, families mirror the wider society and as the countries are altered and forced to adapt to demographic changes, and as institutions become stressed by these changes, the family will consequently be transformed for better or for worse. The restructuring of family life further reflects shifts in consciousness away from traditional mass consciousness toward greater individualism and self-direction.

STUDY QUESTIONS

1. There is a debate as to whether the family in the United States is in a state of crisis, or whether it is undergoing a fundamental transition. Discuss these two positions and on that basis, render an opinion.
2. What are the benefits and drawbacks to monogamy and polygamy as it is practiced in the world today?
3. Discuss the strengths and weaknesses of authoritarian parenting, hyperparenting, and permissive parenting. Which style of parenting do you think is the most effective, and why?

Figure Credits

CHAPTER FOURTEEN

Political Power & Authority

WHAT IS POLITICS? The standard definition of **politics** concerns *the activities associated with the governance of a country or other area*. Particularly, this involves debate or conflict among individuals or parties having or hoping to achieve power.[1] The key term is *governance*, which has to do with the way organizations and countries are managed. It would be hard to imagine a society without some sort of governance, which would be a condition of **anarchy**, meaning *a state of disorder due to absence or non-recognition of authority*. Underscoring politics are the fundamental ideas of power and authority. **Power** rests upon *the ability to achieve desired ends despite resistance from others*. In other words, it is a form of coercion. Power can be exercised in three ways: first, by the use of physical force through police and military power, second, by means of law, rules, or regulations that are enforced, and thirdly, by established custom, which is adherence to long-established norms. For power to be effective, it must rest upon a degree of **authority**, which is *power that people perceive as legitimate*. **Legitimacy** is *the belief that a rule, institution, or leader has the right to govern*. Under normal circumstances, people may not like politicians, the laws they enact, and the policies they put in place, but few will question their right to govern or the legitimacy of the institution of government. One might say, therefore that when it comes to governance, authority is the carrot and power is the stick.

Power and authority are expressions of consciousness, since both terms are manifestations of certain kinds of energy. Power is the forceful energy of one's personality, which is often directive and purposeful. Hence, power is the means to enforce, manage, and dominate others. Likewise, authority is an attractive consciousness that relates, integrates, and usually glamorizes the personality of the one holding power.

---

1 Oxford Living Dictionaries, s.v. "politics," https://en.oxforddictionaries.com/definition/politics.

TYPES OF AUTHORITY

There are broadly three kinds of authority. The first, **traditional authority**, is *a type of authority that has stood the test of time. Its authority is largely tied to tradition or custom.* Traditional authority in sociological terms is the first of Max Weber's three-fold classification of authority. The royal family in Great Britain symbolizes a form of traditional authority even though the role of the monarch is mostly ceremonial with very little real power. Societies which possess a form of traditional authority may be immersed with religion. Saudi Arabia, for example, is an Islamic theocratic monarchy. The Sunni form of Islam is the official state religion. The legal basis of religion and government is Sharia law and non-Muslims are forbidden to hold Saudi citizenship.

Weber's next classification of authority is **rational-legal authority**. This is based on the belief that *the legal structure of society and appointed or elected officials hold legitimate positions.* The majority of the modern states of the twentieth and twenty-first centuries are based on rational-legal authorities. Countries included in this classification range from so-called democracies that exist in North America and Western Europe to more authoritarian regimes, for example, China. In each case there is a legal basis for the exercise of power and authority.

The third and last classification of authority is **charismatic authority**, which *rests "on devotion to the exceptional sanctity, heroism or exemplary character of an individual person."*[2] In fact, most famous people have some measure of charismatic authority. One can think of numerous persons who possess this form of magnetic appeal, for example Martin Luther King Jr., who was one of the guiding lights of the civil rights movement. Gandhi, John F. Kennedy, and Malcolm X might also be included. Charismatic authority is not only reserved for political and religious leaders but can be found in all walks of life. Think of sports, music, and film stars who naturally by means of their dynamic personalities, or manufactured fame, possess a similar appeal.

POLITICAL SYSTEMS AND THE USE OF POWER

Political forms of government have a correlation with the various types of authority. Essentially, there are five kinds of political systems, which often overlap. It is not often the case that a country will be strictly governed by a single political system. The first is **autocracy**, *a system of government by one person with absolute power.* An autocracy may range from an absolute monarchy to a totalitarian dictatorship. The common thread is that both place absolute power in the hands of a single individual.

---

2   Max Weber, "The Types of Legitimate Domination," in *Sociological Theory in the Classical Era: Text and Readings*, eds. Laura Desfor Edles and Scott Appelrouth (Los Angeles: Sage Publications, 2010), 204.

FIGURE 14.1. Absolute Monarchies and Former British Dominions under the British Constitutional Monarchy around the World.

Next on the list are oligarchy and plutocracy. An **oligarchy** is *a small group of people having control of a country, organization, or institution*. A **plutocracy** is largely the same thing with the slight caveat that *it is government by the wealthy*. These forms of government have become more evident in the modern world as power in many states has become increasingly centralized and remote from its citizens.

When *an extensive group of states or countries come under a single authority* you have an **empire**. Throughout history there have been many empires, including the Roman and Ottoman empires in the past, and the British, American, and Russian empires more recently. Empires may exercise direct (political and economic control), or indirect (proxy) control, which characterizes more recent developments. We will focus more on empires (imperialism) in our next chapter on economics.

A **republic** is where *supreme power rests with the people through their elected representatives, and which has an elected president or prime minister*. A republic is the most inclusive of all the political systems. A society such as the Peoples Republic of China is in many ways an authoritarian oligarchy, yet it also has some characteristics of a republic. The United States, on the other hand, leans towards the more democratic aspects of a republic, but as we shall see, that is only part of the picture. A **democracy** is a form of *government by which the people participate directly, especially through rule of the majority*. By definition, a democracy involves full participation by its citizens.

WHAT IS THE AMERICAN FORM OF GOVERNMENT?

If you were asked the above question, most likely your answer would be that America is a democracy. However, the real answer is far more complex. Constitutionally, the country is a republic since it is a form of indirect governance in which various elected officials represent interests and concerns of the people. This form of government exists in the many clubs, groups, and organizations at the local level where citizens can personally attend meetings, express their wishes and opinions, and participate in decision-making. A democracy is usually characterized by majority rule. America is furthermore a proxy empire based upon a global military presence, often through friendly or client states. The United States has approximately 800 military bases or outposts in over 80 countries. Finally, the country, especially at the national level, operates as a plutocracy. A recent analysis of 534 members of Congress in 2012, based on personal financial disclosure data, estimates that 268 members had a net average worth of $1 million or more. According to a study from the Center for Responsive Politics, a non-partisan watchdog group, most congressional legislators are now millionaires. Wealth attracts wealth, meaning that politicians are far more likely to cater to the interests of wealthy donors and powerful interest groups than those who are not so well-heeled.

AUXILIARY POLITICAL SYSTEMS

There are various organizations and institutions that are not a formal part of government but act within the political system. **Special interest groups** comprise *a group of people or an organization seeking or receiving special advantages, typically through political lobbying.* There are numerous such groups that encompass a variety of business organizations, insurance companies, trade unions, teachers' organizations, health care institutions, religious organization, and many more. The purpose of special interest groups is to educate, influence, and put pressure on governmental bodies so that policies and legislation will benefit the concerns of their members.

Political Action Committees (PACs) are *created by special interest groups to raise money privately so as to influence elections or legislation, especially at the federal level.* PACs operate on a continuous basis but are most active around election time. In the primaries preceding the run-up to the 2016 presidential election, the various candidates raised a total of $1.5 billion to run their campaigns. The amount raised by super PACs was $618 million. The advantage of PACs is that it allows candidates to skirt laws on campaign financing. Since the 2000 election, presidential campaign spending has reached record heights.

POLITICAL IDEOLOGIES

Politics is not just about forms of government, interest groups, and money, it is also about ideas. The terms liberal, conservative, radical, and progressive embody a set of distinctive ideas and policies. For instance, a conservative in American politics will usually favor small government, low taxes, individual liberty, and a strong defense establishment. Liberals, on the other hand, have a more positive attitude towards the role of government, support multi-cultural and social equality, and favor using tax dollars to pay for social programs. Political ideas are not necessarily straightforward insofar as they need to appeal to individuals and voters across a wide spectrum of consciousness, ranging from people who are emotionally-based and do not respond to only vague ideals, to those who are capable of complex thought. Consequently, ideologies are simplified assortments of ideas often appealing to one's desires and self-interest but presented in a coherent fashion.

FIGURE 14.2. Elizabeth Warren, United States Senator and from Massachusetts.

THEORETICAL APPROACHES TO POLITICS

There are two approaches to government, which (as always) conform to our theoretical paradigms. The **pluralist model** *indicates that power is distributed among many groups. These groups may include coalitions of like-minded people, unions, professional associations, and business lobbyists.*[3] According to this model, which is an expression of the structural-functional approach, everyone (theoretically) has some degree of political power, whether individually or as part of an organization. The most fundamental power that a person possesses is the right to vote. Among many so-called western democracies, Americans are less likely to go and vote. Estimates show more than fifty-eight percent of eligible voters went to the polls during the 2016 election, nearly breaking even with the turnout rate set during the last presidential election in 2012.[4] For local elections, the percentage is much smaller, perhaps half that percentage. What this shows is that many people do not exercise their piece of political power, which may be due to apathy or the belief that their vote would make no difference. Not surprisingly, young and poorer people are less likely to vote than older and more

3   "Social Power Theories: Pluralist, Power-Elite & Marxist Models," Study.com, https://study.com/academy/lesson/social-power-theories-pluralist-power-elite-marxist-models.html.

4   Michael D. Regan, "What does voter turnout tell us about the 2016 election?" PBS, November 20, 2016, https://www.pbs.org/newshour/politics/voter-turnout-2016-elections.

affluent voters. The limitation of the pluralist model is that power is not evenly distributed throughout the society.

The other theoretical approach, which is a response to the limitation of the pluralist model, is the **power-elite model**. *This model posits that power rests in the hands of elites.* Even in a representative form of government, elites determine policy, influence the content of laws, and structure public debate. The power-elite model, put forward by sociologist C. Wright Mills, is yet another version of the conflict paradigm. Thus, it assumes that power is unevenly distributed between those at the top of the pyramid, such as corporate, military, and political leaders, along with those commanding the most wealth. In other words, the power-elite model assumes that governments function more as oligarchies and plutocracies than democratic and representative systems. Further down the line are interest group leaders, local public-opinion makers (such as the media), and high-profile activists. At the bottom are the masses of people, unorganized, mostly exploited, and largely disinterested. Clearly, those at the top of the political scale, according to this model, use power to further their own interests, and those who serve their interests, with relatively little regard for the bulk of the population whose concerns are divided. The limitation of the power-elite model is the important role of public opinion, which can often influence and determine laws and policies.

GLOBAL POLITICS AND CONSCIOUSNESS

Global politics refers to *politics on a global scale*. It mostly refers to relations between nation states (countries) or issues relating to all or most of them, such as environmental regulation to tackle global warming, which requires international cooperation. The same is true of nuclear disarmament among other major issues that require the attention of all world powers.

Geopolitics *studies the relationships between separate countries or the political importance of their geographical locations and is a key area of global politics, as international relations affect it profoundly.* It may also refer to the inner-workings of the United Nations, the international body that provides countries with a forum for engagement, and the decision-making in a collective group. For instance, the units of the UN—the General Assembly, Security Council, etc.—which was designed to express the collective will of member countries to make resolutions that are binding on all UN members and countries must follow them. These binding agreements are known as international law that has far-reaching influence on global politics as a whole.

The problem with global politics, as with politics in general, is separative allegiances, identities, and interests that divide political units. The political history of the world parallels to a large degree the collective expansion of consciousness that has evolved from small tribal units, through nations, and the phase of strong national identities that are still with us, towards globalization. Conflicts in the world today

FIGURE 14.3. Anti-War Protest: Alberto Gonzales Confirmation Demonstration.

are essentially conflicts of identity that may be nationalism or of an ethnic, religious nature. In this sense, politics is a psychological matter in which nations and countries operate as individual personalities. Soul-centered politics would imagine the world in terms of a common humanity. Although there has been some movement in this direction, it remains a distant ideal.

While many people might claim to have no interest in politics, we are involved in politics all the time. This is obviously due to the fact that we exercise, consciously or not, power all the time in our daily activities, work or school environment, and particularly in our relationships. Since good government involves the right use of power, so this applies to everyone individually and in their groups and organizations. Hence, politics is far more pervasive than we might think.

STUDY QUESTIONS

1. Discuss some of the ways that the United States could be considered a plutocracy, and empire, a republic, and a democracy (hint-think in terms of the pluralist and the power-elite models)
2. To what extent, in your opinion, is politics becoming more geopolitical and less nationally based? Give examples to support your answer.
3. What are some of the advantages and disadvantages of the traditional, rational–legal, and charismatic types of authority?

Figure Credits

CHAPTER FIFTEEN

The Structure of Economic Life

WHAT IS ECONOMICS? *Economics studies the production, distribution, and consumption of goods and services in a society and between societies.* Economics thereby focuses on the behavior and interactions of economic agents and how economies work. The key phrase is the "interactions of economic agents." This means that economic activity is essentially relational. The production of goods and services often involves the concerted efforts of persons and organizations performing different but cooperative roles. Distribution is the action of sharing something among a number of recipients. Consumption is also a relational activity involving consumer choices and interaction with the provider of goods and services. How well and equitably goods, services, and money flow within and between societies often determines the health and well-being of an industry, service, region, or nation. With this in mind, we will explore the structure of systems that comprise economic life.

HISTORICAL STAGES OF ECONOMIC DEVELOPMENT

Referring back to the model of how societies change as expounded by Gerhard Lenski in Chapter Six, we saw that societies undergo a historical development based on changes in technology. Putting aside the question of whether this is the best explanation for historical change, it does suggest that there are significant revolutions that lead to changes in the economy. For many centuries, life centered around agriculture, which involved growing crops and animal husbandry. Along about the eighteenth century in parts of Europe (particularly Britain), population growth was coupled with increased wealth from the expansion of trade and commerce. These provided an environment for the invention of new machinery, particularly in the textile industry, that was the impetus for the industrial revolution, reaching its high point in the late nineteenth and early twentieth centuries. After the Second World War (1939–1945), new advances in science and technology led to the creation of the computer, which although large, slow, and relatively primitive at first, developed exponentially over a very short time into the information revolution of today. The pace of economic growth coupled with technological knowledge promises to re-order societies in ways that now seem barely imaginable.

SECTORS OF THE ECONOMY

Economic development involves a three-stage process. The first is the **primary sector** which relates to *materials from the natural environment*. The products we purchase, and use come from a natural source, or comprise materials from the natural environment. Houses are often built from trees made into lumber, food comes from animal and plant life, and so the list goes on. Once material is derived from the primary sector, it then needs to be *transformed into manufactured goods*. This is the **secondary sector**. The production of automobiles involves the use of raw materials from a variety of sources which are brought together to make a single product. While the first two sectors deal with the process of manufacturing, the third or **tertiary sector** relates to the *service-based portion of the economy*. Doctors, lawyers, teachers, retail clerks, nurses, waiters, night club dancers, and many others are service workers who are a vital part of the economy. Fifty years ago, the service sector accounted for about sixty percent of US output and employment. Today, the service sector's share of the US economy has risen to roughly eighty percent.[1]

THE EVOLUTION OF EXCHANGE SYSTEMS

Money is the concretized expression of a type of energy whose value is determined by people's needs and desires. Essentially, it is an attractive energy that flows naturally to those persons and institutions who have the will and power to direct it to their purposes for good or evil.

Historical changes in the production of goods, services, and technology correspond to the evolution of monetary systems. **Money** is *a medium of exchange, usually in the form of coins and banknotes*. A **medium of exchange** is *a tradeable entity used to avoid the inconveniences of a pure barter system*. This permits the value of goods to be assessed and rendered in terms of an intermediary system, most often a form of money widely accepted to buy any other product. In itself, forms of money have no intrinsic value and only has a worth based upon what a society deems its value should be. Early money consisted almost exclusively of metal coins and other physical

---

1   US Department of Commerce. "The Role of Services in the Modern U.S. Economy," January 1999, https://www.trade.gov/td/sif/PDF/ROLSERV199.PDF.

materials. As economies expanded, particularly with the coming of the industrial age, paper bills of exchange came into use so as to facilitate the flow of goods and services. More recently, financial transactions involve wide scale transfers so that exchanges take place without any tangible resources. The most recent virtual currency is **Bitcoin**, introduced in 2008, which is essentially *computer code backed by no government and has a fluctuating value linked in part to a scarcity that is mathematically predetermined.* Unlike other forms of digital cash, bitcoin is truly untraceable and therefore cannot be recovered if lost or destroyed.[2] Such forms of exchange represent a radical departure from that of the past, as the economy becomes increasingly global.

ECONOMIC SYSTEMS

There are essentially two kinds of economic systems in the world today, which include within them many variations. The first is **capitalism**. This is *an economic system in which natural resources and the means of producing goods and services are privately owned.* The key words here are privately owned. This means that the economy in a capitalist society is largely owned and run by individuals, corporations, or other institutions, apart from the state. The purest form of capitalism is **laissez-faire** in which *owners of businesses and corporations exercise a free hand to control their organization as they see fit, without any governmental interference.* This is also referred to as free-market capitalism, based solely on the supply and demand for goods and services. Laissez-faire capitalism has its political counterpart in libertarianism based on complete freedom of choice, autonomy, and voluntary association.

At the other end of the capitalist spectrum is what might be referred to as **welfare state capitalism.** This form of capitalism is *a system whereby the government undertakes to protect the health and well-being of its citizens, especially those in financial or social need, by means of grants, pensions, and other benefits.*[3] The foundations were laid for the modern welfare state in the US by New Deal programs implemented by the administration of President Franklin D. Roosevelt. His program for social security provided a form of old-age pensions, along with workman's compensation, and aid to impoverished families with children. The welfare state expanded in the 1960s with the addition of Medicare and Medicaid, government healthcare programs, among other social benefits. Two other variations of capitalism include **welfare capitalism**, which is *the practice of businesses providing welfare services to their employees,* and **state capitalism**, or *a system in which the state has control of production and the use of capital.*

---

2 *Merriam-Webster,* s.v. " bitcoin," https://www.merriam-webster.com/dictionary/Bitcoin.

3 Oxford Living Dictionaries, s.v. "welfare state," https://en.oxforddictionaries.com/definition/welfare_state.

FIGURE 15.1. Trump is the Symptom, Capitalism is the Disease, Socialism is the Cure.

The alternative to capitalism is **socialism.** Socialism is defined as *an economic system in which natural resources and the means of producing goods and services are collectively owned.* You can see that this definition parallels that of capitalism except for the interchange of the words *collectively* owned for *privately* owned. Collective ownership is ownership of the means of production by all members of a group for the benefit of all its members. Thus, socialism may apply on the micro-level to a food co-op where customers may own part of a business and share in the profits. On the macro-level, socialism may refer to a society where utilities and industries that produce essential services are owned and run by the government. At the same time there is some degree of private ownership. Often socialist societies provide, through taxes, free services to its citizens such as health care, day care for children, and education, while greatly subsidizing the cost of food, transportation, and other such things. This is characteristic of many economies in Western Europe, often referred to as mixed economies.

An extreme form of socialism is **communism**, which is *a society in which all property is publicly owned, and each person works and is paid according to their abilities and needs.* While communism in theory might offer an ideal social arrangement, efforts to implement the sort of communism envisioned by Karl Marx has been buttressed by brutal dictatorships of which the Soviet Union was a prime example.

THE GLOBAL ECONOMY

Globalization, or the *elimination of barriers to trade, communication, and cultural exchange* is a reality today in the economic life of the planet. The global economy essentially involves economic activity that crosses borders. This brings into play a variety of factors including a global division of labor whereby the making of a product, such as automobiles, involves workers producing parts for a car in different countries. International trade, which goes without saying, is another factor, as is the dominance of multi-national corporations. A **corporation** is *a company or group of people authorized to act as a single entity (legally a person) and recognized as such in law.* As economies expand beyond their national borders, many corporations have formed into monopolies or oligopolies, meaning a state of limited competition, in which a market is shared by a small number of producers or sellers.[4] The dominance by large economic units on the global stage has led to a number of problems such as conflicting laws and regulations among member states that affect trade, diverse environmental standards, concerns over worker's rights, and income standards. According to the World Bank, the richest countries in the world control over seventy-nine percent of the global income compared to around five percent for low-income countries.

Another consequence of globalization relates to standardization that has been referred to by sociologist George Ritzer as the McDonaldization model, named after the global fast food chain. The elements of this model are 1) efficiency or finding the most effective operating procedures, 2) calculability, which is rationalization and scientific management, 3) predictability, meaning that everything looks and tastes the same, and finally, 4) control through non-human technology, which is the application of information systems and decentralized management to production and labor issues.

Globalization has complicated and exacerbated the issue of free trade vs. protectionism. **Free trade** is *international trade left to its natural course without tariffs, quotas, or other restrictions.*[5] While free trade is designed to create open markets and thus enhance wealth and living standards of countries sharing such agreements, it has also given a boost to the influence of large corporations, which often use their power to exploit and run roughshod over resource-rich poorer countries and indigenous peoples.

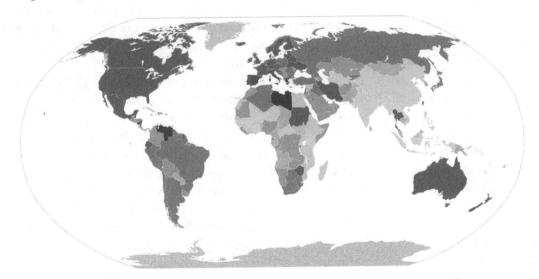

FIGURE 15.2. Map of Projected Real GDP Growth Rate in 2020—Dark Green Signifies Positive Growth and Dark Red Signifies Negative Growth.

4   Oxford Living Dictionaries, s.v. "oligopoly," https://en.oxforddictionaries.com/definition/oligopoly.

5   Oxford Living Dictionaries, s.v. "free trade," https://en.oxforddictionaries.com/definition/free_trade.

Protectionism, on the other hand, is *the theory or practice of shielding a country's domestic industries from foreign competition by taxing imports.*[6] Countries often engage in protectionist practices for political reasons and to punish other states for engaging in unfair trade and financial practices. While protectionism leading to trade wars may bring short-term benefits to a particular country, in the long-term such practices have been demonstrated to be harmful and ineffective.

THEORETICAL MODELS OF GLOBALIZATION

There are two economic models that have been developed to explain the relation between rich and poor countries within the global economy. The first is **modernization theory,** which *is a model used to explain why some societies develop economically and why other societies are left behind. Modernization explains the gap that exists between a "pre-modern" or "traditional" society and one that is modern.* This theory, developed by social scientists in the 1950s, argues that the goal for under-developed societies is to follow the path taken by richer nations.

The economist W.W. Rostow laid down four stages in this process. The first is what he called the traditional stage, whereby an agricultural-based society resists changes to its way of life. The second stage is the take-off phase when, through an influx of outside capital and entrepreneurial activity, the society undergoes a period of rapid economic growth. Thirdly, so the theory goes, the society reaches the stage of maturation. It is here that the economy of a less-developed nation becomes integrated into the global economy and where modern industrial systems are firmly implanted. The final stage is that of mass production and mass consumption in which wages rise and the demand and manufacture of vast consumer goods is prevalent.

Modernization theory posits that rich nations have an important role to play by helping poorer nations to control population growth which is most prevalent in the less-developed regions of the world. Also, modernization is said to increase food production through the introduction of manufactured seeds and fertilizers, and through the utilization of industrial technology. Finally, rich countries are said to assist poorer countries through non-military foreign aid by means of government contracts, given to corporations to implement large capital projects that favor the rich nations as well.

While some countries have benefitted from this model, many others have not or could not follow this pattern for cultural or political reasons. Rich countries operate from a position of strength. Much like a monopoly game, those with the most resources are generally the winners. Furthermore, there is an ethnocentric bias to modernization theory implying that poor countries are responsible for their poverty. Since rich industrialized countries are the greatest contributors to global warming,

---

6   Oxford Living Dictionaries, s.v. "protectionism," https://en.oxforddictionaries.com/definition/protectionism.

pollution, and other environmental hazards, it is debatable whether modernization theory could ever lead to a sustainable planet.

The counter argument to modernization theory is **dependency theory**, which explains *global inequality in terms of the historical exploitation of poor societies by those that are rich.*[7] According to the **world systems theory**, an approach to world history and social change developed by sociologist Immanuel Wallerstein, *there is a world economic system in which some countries benefit while others are exploited.* This form of exploitation is based on capitalism. Accordingly, rich countries impose conditions of dependency on poorer nations by forcing nations with narrow export economies to compete on the global market against more sophisticated and diverse economies. Poorer countries also lack the industrial capacity of richer nations. In order to compete, less-developed countries are often forced to borrow from international lending organizations like the World Bank and the International Monetary Fund. Often the inability to pay back loans leads to further borrowing and more poverty. It is like using your credit card to pay for essential services, resulting in a debt trap.

Dependency theory looks at the unequal power relations that have developed as a result of colonialism. **Colonialism** has been around for centuries and is *the process by*

FIGURE 15.3. McDonald's Restaurant in Qatar.

---

7   Maqbool Ahmad, *Dictionary of Education* (New Delhi: Atlantic Publishers & Dist, 2008), 143.

which some nations enrich themselves through political and economic control of other nations. The British and French Empires of the eighteenth and nineteenth centuries are a case in point. More recently, a new form of global power relationships has emerged called **neocolonialism.** *It involves not direct political control but exploitation by multinational corporations.* Neocolonialism is often buttressed by proxy imperialism, or the establishment of friendly governments to protect the corporate interests of a developed country. The desire by rich nations to covet the resources of poorer nations, often through the use of military force, has led to much conflict and destabilization in the world.

While dependency theory goes a long way toward explaining the unequal relations between rich and poor nations, it does have some limitations. The principal criticism of dependency theory has been that it does not provide any substantive empirical evidence to support its arguments. There are few obvious examples but also many exceptions that do not fit the theory. Examples include the newly emerged industrial countries of Southeast Asia and the Middle East. At the same time, dependency theory is short on solutions to the problem of global poverty as opposed to the explanation provided by modernization theory.

The importance of economics in the world today cannot be overstated. Not only is it at the root of many social problems such as poverty and unemployment, but it often dominates the thinking and choices made by governments, corporations and small businesses, other for-profit and nonprofit organizations, and individual families. As social consciousness expands, there is a greater demand that economic decisions involve values such as equality and fairness that relate to the greatest good for the greatest number of people. Such is the expression of soul energy into the economic sphere.

STUDY QUESTIONS

1. Discuss the relative merits and demerits of socialism and capitalism. Can these two economic systems function simultaneously in the same society?

2. To what extent is the relationship between rich and poorer countries characterized by Modernization Theory and Dependency Theory? Explain each theory and give specific examples in support of your answer.

3. Discuss some of the ways information technology is transforming the industrial economy into a new kind of society? What are some of the benefits and shortcomings of this transition?

Figure Credits

CHAPTER SIXTEEN

Religion & Spirituality

WHAT IS RELIGION and spirituality and what is the distinction between these two terms? **Religion** may be defined as *the belief in and worship of a superhuman controlling power, especially a personal God or gods.*[1] **Spirituality**, on the other hand, refers to *the quality of being concerned with the human spirit or soul as opposed to material or physical things.*[2] Clearly there is a difference. Religion relates to a variety of sectarian beliefs centered on peculiar dogmas, rituals, and often scriptures that originated in various cultures and in different parts of the world. Spirituality pertains to the core values and esoteric principles that lie at the root of all organized religions. Generally speaking, most religions are concerned with the moral improvement of its members and establishing a relationship with a god or deities however characterized and defined. Spirituality is a much broader concept and relates to the non-material realm of spiritual experience or causes. One might say, therefore, that religion involves the connection of the human personality to the unseen realm of mystical beings or the effects of spiritual forces. Spirituality, on the other hand, concerns the life of the soul and its corresponding impact on human affairs, individually and collectively. Crudely put, spirituality is a top-down expression of consciousness, and religion is a bottom up approach to the superhuman world.

THE SOCIOLOGICAL PERSPECTIVE OF RELIGION

Since sociologists view religion from the perspective of a social institution, they are concerned with the cultural characteristics of religious experience

---

1 Oxford Living Dictionaries, s.v. "religion," https://en.oxforddictionaries.com/definition/religion.
2 Oxford Living Dictionaries, s.v. "spiritual," https://en.oxforddictionaries.com/definition/spiritual.

and the structure of religious institutions. In sociological terms, religion is a unified system of beliefs and practices relative to sacred things. What is meant by **sacred**? It refers to *any activity set apart as extraordinary, inspiring awe or reverence.* Clearly, this is a very broad definition and could include seeing a beautiful rainbow or having a mystical experience. Essentially, it involves anything that elevates a person to a higher state of awareness or consciousness. The opposite of sacred is **profane**. This term has several meanings but the most relevant one concerns something that is secular or materialistic. Since much of our daily existence would be classified as profane, the sacred would be something extraordinary or unusual.

The way of approaching the sacred found in most religions is through ritual. Life is full of many rituals, but in a religious context **ritual** is *formal ceremonial behavior providing a context for inducing the sacred.* Rituals may involve a repetition of words or behaviors, the use of incense, and singing or chanting. The idea is always to elevate a person from the profane to the sacred.

One of the main functions of ritual is to reinforce one's faith. In the context of religion, one can define **faith** as *a strong belief in God or in the doctrines of a religion, based on spiritual apprehension rather than proof.*[3] As mentioned in Chapter Three on critical thinking, belief is the acceptance of a statement as true without evidence of proof. Faith is related to one's level of consciousness. As a person's consciousness expands through critical thinking, their perceptions change along with their beliefs and understanding of reality.

THEORETICAL ANALYSIS

Emile Durkheim annunciated the structural-functional approach to religion. He noted that religion functioned as "a unified system of beliefs and practices relative to sacred things, that is to say, things set apart and forbidden—beliefs and practices which unite in one single moral community."[4] This is accomplished through:

1. Social cohesion which unites a congregation or community of believers around a common set of values and core beliefs that bonds the group together;
2. All religions seek to impose some measure of social control over their members through moral teaching, and in some cases, the threat of divine displeasure. Some religions are involved in social activism and justice related issues, which are interpreted in moral terms.

---

3 Oxford Living Dictionaries, s.v. "faith," https://en.oxforddictionaries.com/definition/faith.

4 "The Elementary Forms of the Religious Life (1912)," Retrieved from http://durkheim.uchicago.edu/Summaries/forms.html.

3. Finally, religions promote cohesion by providing answers to questions that go beyond everyday existence. Where did we come from? Is there life after death? Why is there hardship and suffering? Thus, religions seek to give meaning and purpose to life.

FIGURE 16.1. Idol Image Procession–Greek Orthodox Church in Florida.

The interaction paradigm sees religion as a social construction, insofar as religions are human creations that involve frameworks of comprehension. Thus, religions reinforce shared spheres of understanding through the particular use of symbols, ceremonies, and language. The cross, the yin/yang symbol, and the image of the Buddha sitting on a lotus all convey meaning to persons of a certain faith. Ceremonies such as religious processions and festivals and the celebration of saints days or holy days like Yom Kippur reinforce religious meaning. At the same time, religious organizations have their own jargon, which often arises out of sacred texts and scriptures.

The conflict perspective raises the question of how religion supports social inequality. For one thing, organized religions are by nature conservative and are more likely to support those institutions and forces in society that uphold the status quo. This is particularly true of the so-called fundamentalist religions that base their faith on absolute authority. This explains, for instance, why the so-called evangelical Christian religions in the United States tend to be more politically and socially conservative. The same could be said about the Muslim faith, whether Sunni or Shi'a, or the Hindu and Buddhist religions.

Throughout their history, many conventional religions have had a strong gender bias. Numerous passages from the Christian bible have explicitly or implicitly promoted male dominance. The fact that religious organizations (not all) have been or are hierarchical has had the effect of reinforcing the authority of men over women. This has largely changed among the mainline churches that encourage the ordinations of women and preach social equality.

Karl Marx was quoted as saying that "religion is the opiate of the masses." What he meant by this statement is that religions offer unrealistic "pie in the sky" prospects for a pleasurable afterlife at the expense of combatting injustices in the material world. In this sense, religion operates as a powerful diversion so as to keep people complaisant and subordinate to civil authority. The structural-functional counterargument would be that religion provides comfort, community, and meaning that enrich a person's life.

Given that religion is often the cause of wars and conflict is another issue that a conflict theorist might put forward.

TYPES OF RELIGIOUS ORGANIZATIONS

We often tend to think of religious organizations as churches, mosques, or temples. Religions may be categorized according to the degree of their integration into society. Whereas the formal definition of a church is a building for public and especially Christian worship, from a sociological perspective a **church** is *a religious organization that is highly integrated into society.* This means that it blends in with the dominant culture and is supportive of other social institutions. There are two kinds of churches. A **state church** is a religious body or creed officially endorsed by the state. A state with an official religion is backed by the laws and political power of a nation. Such an example would be the Catholic Church in Costa Rica and Italy or the Muslim religion in Iran. The other type of church is a denomination. A **denomination** is *a form of religious organization that functions independently within a society without interference from the state.* The United States, with its constitutionally mandated separation between church and state, is a prime example of this form of religious organization.

Another form of religion is a **sect**, which *stands apart or is critical of the dominant society.* Some independent religious organizations in the United States, such as the Amish, which sticks to traditional ways and sets themselves apart, would be classified as a sect. Some charismatic churches that form around a dynamic leader and espouse a kind of religion that departs in some ways from conventional Christian teaching would similarly qualify as sects.

The final category of religious organization is a cult. **Cults** are *religions that stand outside the religions of a particular society.* While cults are sometimes seen as weird or demonic, they are usually benign and often quite interesting. So-called **New Age religions** are *loosely knit organizations that often combine practices from various traditions that are not indigenous to a particular society.* Such religions may involve the study of astrology, the practice of using healing crystals, Native American rituals, psychotherapy, yoga, numerology, and meditation. The innovative approaches of such cults may be the bellwether of new ideas that will at some point be incorporated into more established religions. It should be remembered that Christianity started as a cult before becoming a sect and later a religion.

ELEMENTS OF SPIRITUALITY

The search for spirituality takes many forms and is a prevalent social movement in a number of countries. Essentially, it is a quest for the experience of the soul. A prominent method for achieving access to higher forms of consciousness is through meditation. Meditation is defined as *achieving a relaxed and constant state of inner quiet so as to acquire some insight or revelation.* Many Eastern religions such as Buddhism and Hinduism place meditation at the core of their rituals and practices. Prayer is also an avenue for connection with one's soul. In some quarters there has been a renewed interest in ancient mystery schools, Freemasonry, and the early origins of contemporary religions that contain much hidden wisdom. With the expansion of eastern religions and occult ideas into the West, a greater emphasis has been placed on developing a person's higher mental faculties and less on mysticism and emotional faith, thus the importance of critical thinking.

RELIGION AND SOCIAL CHANGE

While religions often resist change, certain social movements have greatly impacted religious consciousness. Max Weber hypothesized a correlation between the emergence of Protestantism in the sixteenth century and capitalism. According to his argument, the same virtues of independence, self-help, thriftiness, hard work, and prosperity, which have been identified with the rise of capitalism, were the same as those favored by Protestants (Calvinists) who combined worldly success with the promise of spiritual reward in the afterlife. What is implied is that various institutions (religion and economics in this case) reinforce the alteration of other institutions when conditions are conducive.

During the 1960s, **liberation theology** began as *a movement in Christian theology, developed mainly by Latin American Roman Catholics, that emphasizes liberation from*

FIGURE 16.2. Support of Political Activism by Church Groups.

social, political, and economic oppression as an anticipation of ultimate salvation.[5] Characteristically, liberation theology was most influential among priests who served the poor in their parishes and saw that the Christian message of love and the exaltation of the poor were compatible with the Marxist idea of class struggle. Liberation theology is less prominent today but still has a number of followers.

Black liberation theology emerged as a doctrine in black churches during the struggle against segregation in the United States. Similar to liberation theology, **black liberation theology** sees *the Christian message as compatible with the struggle for equal justice and civil rights.* This perspective has also been adopted by religious organizations who view social issues as an important aspect of their faith. In other respects, black religious organizations have doctrines and beliefs similar to other Christian churches.

---

5   Oxford Living Dictionaries, s.v. "liberation theology," http://oxforddictionaries.com/us/definition/american_english/liberation%2Btheology.

WORLD RELIGIONS

The major world religions while distinctive in terms of dogmas and belief systems, share certain doctrines and cultural similarities. Essentially, these religions can be grouped according to the geographic regions where they emerged. The first of these three groups is the western religions. These include Christianity, Islam, and Judaism. These three religions are all monotheistic, meaning that they believe in one supreme deity that is the creator and ruler of the universe. By the same token, these religions emerged in the Middle East, trace their roots back to Abraham, believe in the historical existence of Jesus, focus on the individual within a spiritual community, see history in a linear fashion as having a point of creation and a conclusion at the end of time, and hold to a doctrine of judgement and redemption.

The religions of South Asia (Buddhism and Hinduism) emphasize great cycles of time as opposed to the linear development that is accepted by the western religions. The law of cycles holds that people are subject to reincarnation and karma. This book accepts the assumption that reincarnation and karma are fundamental characteristics of the human condition. Consequently, men and women live countless lives from which they gain much experience and wisdom. Karma is the ethical rule which states that for every action there is a corresponding reaction, which crudely put is a system of rewards and punishments. Hinduism is one of the world's oldest religions and was a synthesis of a number of Indian sects and cults. Buddhism grew out of the Hindu tradition. Founded by Siddhartha Gautama after his achieved enlightenment, this religion is said to be approximately 1,500 years old.

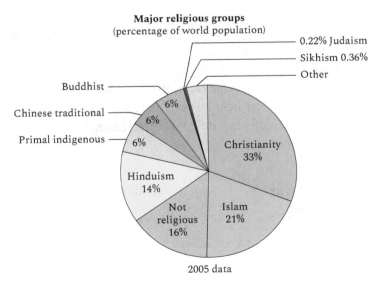

Major religious groups
(percentage of world population)

0.22% Judaism
Sikhism 0.36%
Other

Buddhist

Chinese traditional

Primal indigenous

6%
6%
6%

Christianity
33%

Hinduism
14%

Not
religious
16%

Islam
21%

2005 data

FIGURE 16.3. Major Religions – 2005 Pie Chart.

The religions of Eastern Asia, Confucianism and Taoism, are in effect schools of philosophy dealing with the question of how to achieve social harmony. In this respect they are the most sociological of all the major religions. It is by employing the eight virtues of both religions, namely filial piety, sibling harmony, dedication, trustworthiness, propriety, sacrifice, honor, and sense of shame that accordingly we become fully human. Practicing the virtues is integral to Confucian and Taoist training. Aside from cultivating virtue, Confucianism and Taoism honor various deities and engage in rituals, meditation, and various ceremonies to connect with the spiritual world. Religious practice within the East Asian religions is less sectarian than in the West, and Confucianism, Taoism, and Buddhism often overlap and borrow from each other.

The fact that all religions grew up in certain localities and are bounded by a particular culture accounts for their apparent distinctiveness. There is evidence to show that as countries become more affluent, they become more secular. Religion, however, is fundamental to all societies, which makes it an essential component to the human experience. From an evolutionary perspective, religion is about the maturation of consciousness from the viewpoint of seeing truth in one religion, or a denomination of that one religion, to an understanding that there are many paths to truth and that individual faiths are only streams into the ocean of spiritual reality. In the words of the apostle Paul, "faith is the substance of things hoped for, the evidence of things not seen" (Hebrews 11:1). The faith that he is talking about is seeing into the realm of the soul beyond the world of matter or form.

STUDY QUESTIONS

1. Discuss what is meant by spirituality and religion. Can one be spiritual without being religious and vice versa?
2. Discuss the basic differences between a church, a domination, a sect, and a cult. Can it be said that all major religions were initially cults?
3. Can religious organizations best be seen as socially functional, as reinforcing social inequality, or as defining cultural differences?

Figure Credits

CHAPTER SEVENTEEN

Education & Schooling

WHAT IS EDUCATION? This term comes from the root word *educere* meaning to bring out or lead forth. Said otherwise, the implied meaning of education is *to elaborate, and clarify what already exists.* Such a definition may appear odd, but people have accumulated lots of skills and knowledge over many lifetimes in varying rates of development according to one's level of consciousness. Thus, while education is seemingly about learning new things, it is built upon a foundation of existing knowledge. This is why many of us pick up a subject or skill very quickly but may struggle with other branches of learning.

Looking at more recent definitions, it is important to distinguish between what is meant by education and training. **Education** is *the process of facilitating learning, or the acquisition of knowledge, skills, values, beliefs, and habits.* To a large extent, education is about learning one's culture and the facets of one's civilization. **Training** is *the teaching or developing skills and knowledge that relates to specific useful competencies.* In other words, education deals with broad theoretical issues across a range of disciplines, whereas training is about learning specific processes necessary to complete a task or function. Through our interactions with others, we are constantly gaining useful knowledge and skills directly or indirectly. **Schooling**, on the other hand, involves *formal instruction by trained teachers.* Obviously, schooling is only part of one's total learning experience.

FUNCTIONS OF EDUCATION

Since education sociologically is studied within an institutional structure, our discussion of education (and training) will be within the context of schooling. The objective of education is to connect students with their culture, which of course involves learning specific fields of study. The primary grades focus on basic literacy, numeracy, social skills, and, the teaching of norms and values, which is important for integrating one into the civilized order of any society.

This is referred to as the **hidden curriculum,** defined as *a latent or unintended aspect of an education. It involves the transmission of norms and values that are an important part of socialization but are not part of any set curriculum.* That said, the hidden curriculum provides the structure for learning to take place and is an essential facet of education. Secondary education further probes culture through an investigation of ideas, technical processes, and the meanings that they convey. Teaching at this level seeks to show connections that exist within specific fields of knowledge, and to some extent between fields of knowledge. Beyond high school, further study in theoretical disciplines becomes more specialized often leading to new discoveries or the validation of existing "truths." In terms of training, one is taught to master more complex problems and processes. Ultimately, the goal of education is to further the evolution of the human race, which is another way of looking at spirituality.

THEORETICAL APPROACHES TO EDUCATION

With respect to educational institutions, the structural-functional perspective maintains that schools and colleges provide the necessary skills and knowledge for a society to function. One such function, as stated earlier, is socialization, which is the ongoing process of cultural learning and self-discovery that is reinforced by family and other institutions. Cultural learning is about the acquisition of useful knowledge that can be applied to self-understanding, a comprehension of issues related to the human experience, or skills that are useful in the workplace.

Schools and colleges indirectly contribute to social integration, meaning the bringing together of kids from diverse backgrounds into a common environment. Since the United States is increasingly becoming a multi-cultural society, there is a need for students to experience a diverse array of social interactions regarding racial, class, and gender.

An important offshoot of education is social placement. One's level of educational achievement is the most important factor in determining his or her status in society. Much of this relates to occupational status, ranging across white-collar and blue-collar jobs. Consequently, there are great disparities of income. Numerous studies have shown that the salary differential between high school and college graduates, not to mention those with advanced post-graduate degrees, has been expanding over the past several decades. This gap will widen even further as students are challenged to have more complex technical skills and theoretical knowledge in order to function in an evolving digital economy.

Finally, there are certain latent functions of education that have unintended consequences. One goes to college usually with the intent of engaging in a field of study or activity, and to obtain a degree in some area. These are manifest functions. At the same time, there are latent functions. Attending college will allow one to meet new people, do things you never anticipated doing, and perhaps meet the love of your life. Hence, education is not just about going to class and studying.

FIGURE 17.1. Classroom of Nursing Students at Univ. of Texas-Arlington.

The conflict perspective states that educational institutions perpetuate and solidify social inequality. This raises a fundamental philosophical question regarding democratic and hierarchical approaches to education. Democracy is about treating everyone equally through directing teaching towards a common standard. The hierarchical approach is to structure educational systems to meet the graded abilities of students based on aptitude and level of consciousness. Whereas democracy in education is about fairness, its drawback is the tendency towards mediocrity. The problem with the hierarchical approach is often favoring the best, the brightest, and the most well-placed students at the expense of those less able and qualified.

Since social institutions tend to be hierarchical, hence unequal, the conflict paradigm usually takes a critical approach to education. The argument is that such practices as tracking or placing students in classes predicated upon their perceived abilities, and utilizing standardized tests, which is a form of stratification that is biased against minority students, undermines the goal of providing everyone with a quality education. Moreover, the inequality between schools based on disproportionate public spending and location further erodes efforts to provide equality in education. Added to this is the fact that money often determines whether a child can afford specialized or private schools, a good college (or college at all), and receive the resources necessary for achieving academic success. Whereas over eighty percent of students in the United States graduate from high school, under twenty-five percent complete a four-year college degree, and a far smaller percentage ends up with post-graduate degrees that enable one to enjoy better pay and a higher status.

The interaction paradigm is about how teachers and school officials define students in terms of academic performance and social class. While the general impression is that education is a meritocracy, personal decisions often play a big role in determining how students are treated and their consequent opportunities. Like anyone else, teachers and administrators prefer some students over others which may translate into skewed perceptions of academic ability. Behavior patterns are also influential factors. Furthermore, racial and ethnic biases may contribute to why some students are left behind. The point is that the mix of perceptions involved in the interactions between students, teachers, and school officials creates a reality that often colors student's abilities and performance.

FIGURE 17.2. Independence High School Graduation.

ISSUES IN SCHOOLS

Schools continue to be affected by issues that are often politically driven. One such matter is school choice. Some have suggested that parents should be allowed to send their children to the school of their choice even though it is outside their local school district. Advocates claim that freedom of choice will allow one to shop for the best educational opportunity and thus force schools to improve through competition. Opponents argue that the end result would be a two-tiered public-school system, which would effectively allow some schools to attract the best students while leaving many others in a worse situation.

Another matter concerns the teaching of religion in schools. The US Constitution and Supreme Court decisions have prohibited schools from establishing or promoting any religion in the public sphere. Questions, however, arise as to what constitutes the teaching of religion, or if any reference to religion is acceptable. This is particularly the case where there is strong sentiment in a community for a particular religion.

Education is one sphere where the battle over the role of religion in a secular society continues to be waged.

Technology has raised some questions as to the mode of teaching. Information technology has enabled students to learn at a distance without being present in a classroom. While this has allowed students to pursue an education more easily within their own circumstances, it has raised questions as to the quality of education and the appropriateness of various courses to this mode of learning. The COVID-19 pandemic has severely disrupted education, making distance learning at least a temporary reality in many places. College administrators often see online courses as a way of increasing student enrollment and reducing costs.

Another factor in higher education has been the emergence of for-profit colleges. These institutions are run like a private business by which colleges (vendors) provide an educational service to consumers (students). While this model can be challenged on philosophic grounds, it is also true that the approach of such colleges has been to recruit low-income students. Consequently, for-profit colleges have laid claim to a lion's share of government grants and student loans, meaning that they are dependent upon public funds for their survival. Questions remain as to whether such institutions serve the students' best interests.

By law, schools and colleges are required to make accommodation for students with disabilities. This may mean allowing students extra time to complete exams or tasks, providing separate learning spaces, developing one-on-one teaching modules, using learning technologies such as computerized voice-recording devices, and other human resources to meet the needs of those who require such help.

ALTERNATIVE APPROACHES TO TRADITIONAL EDUCATION

Whereas over ninety percent of school children attend public schools, a small but significant percentage attends what might be termed alternative schools. One form of education geared particularly towards younger children is Montessori Schools. These schools tend to focus on experiential learning by nurturing a child's curiosity and interest through a flexible curriculum. Along somewhat similar lines are Waldorf Schools. Waldorf education is based on a philosophy known as anthroposophy. Its pedagogy emphasizes the role of imagination in learning, adopting a spiritual approach, and striving to integrate holistically the intellectual, practical, and artistic development of pupils. For a variety of reasons some parents have decided to homeschool their children. As of 2016, there are about 2.3 million homeschooled students in the United States. On average, homeschoolers score at or above the national average on standardized tests. Critics of homeschooling claim that students lack necessary social skills.[1]

---

1   "Fast Facts," Institute of Education Sciences, National Center for Educational Statistics, https://nces.ed.gov/fastfacts/display.asp?id=91.

FIGURE 17.3. Montessori Early Childhood Student, International School.

PROBLEMS IN SCHOOLS

Schools to a large extent reflect problems within society. A major problem in the United States has been school shootings, sometimes on a mass scale. The killing of seventeen students at the Marjory Stoneman Douglas High School in Parkland Florida in February 2018 highlighted a string of such tragic events that have occurred in recent years, and unfortunately continue to happen. Between the years 2010 and 2014 there were ninety-three shootings in and around schools and colleges. Schools have confronted this problem in various ways. The bottom line has been increased security, from having well-placed metal detectors to armed guards or police patrolling school halls and grounds.

Many schools experience a variety of disciplinary problems. Bullying is a common predicament in schools, sometimes with serious consequences. Thousands of students skip school every day for fear of being bullied. According to one survey, sixty percent of middle school students reported having been bullied, while many teachers and staff tend to believe that bullying is far less prevalent. Social media has exacerbated this problem, causing in few instances the victims to commit suicide.

Based on a study by the Council of State Governments Justice Center and the Public Policy Research Institute at Texas A & M University, nearly sixty percent of public junior high school and high school students get suspended or expelled each year, according to a report that tracked about one million Texas children over six years. More than thirty percent of the Texas seventh- through twelfth-grade students receive out-of-school suspension, which averaged two days.[2] Those who have multiple suspensions are more likely to drop out of school or end up in the juvenile justice system.

The quality of education across the United States has also raised some concerns. According to a 2016 survey of thirty-five countries by the Organization for Economic Cooperation and Development (OECD),[3] the United States ranked fourteenth in reading and math scores behind such countries as South Korea, Finland, Canada, and New Zealand. Taking the Finnish school system as an example, there are few if any exams for students well into their teens, virtually no homework, more recess time, and no mandatory testing. At the same time, Finland spends less on students than does the United States and by comparison, more students graduate from high school and go to college. Also, a large number of students go to vocational schools. While educational policy in the United States is determined at the state level and is therefore a mixed bag, the educational success of Finnish schools offers some sound ideas of how American schools might improve, not the least of which are fewer bureaucratic controls and providing greater rewards for teachers.

GLOBAL EDUCATION

Educational inequality around the world remains a serious problem, particularly in certain regions. According to a study by UNESCO,[4] out of a total of 263 million children not in school worldwide, 61 million primary age children in 2016 were not enrolled in school. Of these, forty-seven percent never expected to enter school and twenty-six percent entered but left school for various reasons. Those children living in sub-Saharan Africa are most likely to be excluded from school. Children living in rural areas are twice as likely to be out of school compared to children in urban environments. There is also inequality based on gender. Girls constitute a slight majority of children not in school, whereas two-thirds of illiterate people in the world are women. Cultural norms in many countries often relegate girls to subservient and domestic roles which work against their being educated. The consequence of poor or non-existent educational opportunities is a high rate of illiteracy. Illiteracy is most acute in Africa where less than fifty percent of the population can read or write.

---

2   Gary Scharrer and Jennifer R. Lloyd, "60 percent of Texas students get suspended, expelled," *My San Antonio*, July 19, 2011, https://www.mysanantonio.com/news/education/article/60-percent-of-Texas-students-get-suspended-1471692.php.

3   "Comparison with Other Nations," United Health Foundation, https://www.americashealthrankings.org/learn/reports/%E2%80%A6/comparison-with-other-nation.

4   "263 Million Children and Youth Are Out of School," UNESCO, July 15, 2016, http://uis.unesco.org/en/news/263-million-children-and-youth-are-out-school.

By contrast, many Asian countries display a high degree of educational success. A large percentage of East Asian countries, which account for the majority of nations with high average performance, also see the lowest percentage of low-performing students. This is far better across the board than performances by American students. The difference may in part be attributed to rigorous expectations and cultural factors that propel and focus Asian students to excel.[5] More open educational opportunities and diverse curriculums in western countries at the college level, particularly the United States, have attracted large number of students from around the world who otherwise have fewer alternatives to pursue higher education.

Educational success or failure goes far beyond what is taught in schools and colleges and must be seen within the context of other institutions. The intellectual abilities and quality of expectations within a family translate into a child's academic performance, as does economic and social standing, and focal point of consciousness. By the same token, degrees of functionality or dysfunction within a society can often be traced back to the effectiveness of educational institutions to raise standards, civilize, enculturate, and provide children a vision for the future.

STUDY QUESTIONS

1. Give some reasons why you think that the United States, the richest country in the world, should have such a mediocre educational system compared to some other countries in Asia and Europe?
2. Compare and contrast the three theoretical paradigms with respect to education. Which of these paradigms offers the best explanation of the state of American education today?
3. Discuss the merits and demerits of an educational system that offers two-tiered schools, one for theoretical learning and the other for trade and vocational learning, as opposed to a comprehensive system providing the same education for everyone.

---

5 "Asian Countries Take the U.S. to School," The Atlantic, February 29, 2016, https://www.theatlantic.com/education/archive/2016/02/us-asia-education-differences/471564/

CHAPTER EIGHTEEN

Health & Medicine

WHAT IS HEALTH? **Health** is defined as *the state of being free from illness or injury.* This is probably how we commonly think of health. However, it has a metaphoric meaning as well. People talk about a healthy society or a healthy family meaning a state of well-being, or a condition of wholeness. Wholeness is characterized by the harmonious integration of all the parts within a given system. In a spiritual context, wholeness is an expression of soul light that draws all life-infused substance into a condition of unity. This helps explain why the immune system affords the body protection against disease through natural processes that strives to achieve optimal health, or wholeness. This is true of all forms of life.

From a more mundane and sociological perspective, our discussion will focus on the interaction between society and health. In examining the ways in which health and medicine are rooted in the organization of society, we need to recognize certain basic patterns. The first and obvious point is that cultural patterns define health. While we tend to think that illness and health are universally understood, they are perceived differently according to the norms and values of a given society. For instance, a chest pain in certain western cultures might be perceived as a heart condition, in China the diagnosis could be that the body was overheated causing certain blockages of energy. By the same token, cultural standards change over time. Homosexuality at one time was thought to be a mental illness but today such a notion would be completely discredited.

Secondly, technology affects people's health. Digital scanning devices, lasers, and other diagnostic tools allow for the detection and cure of disease to a far greater extent than would have been possible decades ago. The lack of medical technologies in poorer countries helps explain why the standard of living in such places is far less than in richer nations.

Finally, social inequality affects people's health. People with means can afford better treatment and care than those with fewer resources, especially those living near the subsistence level. Access to healthcare is about social power, which is why it is such a political issue. The debate in the United States over private versus public (state-run) health systems is a case in point.

HISTORICAL PATTERNS OF HEALTH

Taking a simplified historical perspective, patterns of health fit into three distinctive categories. In pre-industrial societies, survival was subject to factors beyond one's control. Many people died as a consequence of continuous warfare, epidemics like the bubonic plague that ravaged whole societies, and frequent famine given that the majority of people were agricultural peasants and were dependent upon the vagaries of weather and other uncontrollable factors.

With the coming of the Industrial Revolution, accompanied by the massing of people together in large cities, contagious diseases such as diphtheria, tuberculosis and influenza laid low many people. Since these diseases were largely due to environmental factors, such as polluted air and water and poor sanitation contributing to epidemics of cholera, pressure was exerted on state and local governments to pass numerous public health laws to combat these problems. Enclosed sewer systems, indoor plumbing, air pollution laws, building codes, and organized street cleaning were positive innovations. The ability to produce a greater variety of foods also contributed to improved nutrition standards. The growth of medical science that made its appearance in the latter half of the nineteenth century enabled doctors to more accurately identify the symptoms of illness and prescribe beneficial remedies. All these factors led to a significant decline in the death rate. Alternative approaches to healing such as homeopathy were also widely used.

Whereas health problems resulted traditionally from environmental factors, illness in the modern world stems primarily from lifestyle patterns. Heart disease, stroke, and various cancers now top the list of serious illnesses brought on by such things as stress, over or wrong eating habits, lack of exercise, and the use of substances such as tobacco, alcohol, and drugs. At the same time, people across the board are living longer with greater vitality and well-being, which indicates that the overall health of humanity continues to improve.

The recent COVID-19 pandemic reminds us that diseases are rarely eradicated and often return in cyclical fashion over a period of time. The Spanish influenza in 1918–1919 killed many more people than those who died during World War I or during the COVID-19 virus. Advances in science, public health, and social awareness have impacted the spread of contagious diseases to some degree.

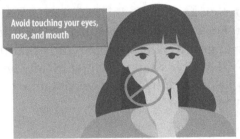
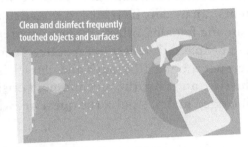

FIGURE 18.1. COVID-19, Stop the Spread of Germs.

HEALTH IN THE UNITED STATES

Social epidemiology refers to the distribution of health and disease across a society's population. This approach gives sociologists an insight as to how illnesses affect distinctive social groups. Illness does not occur randomly but varies according to age, gender, ethnicity, race, geography, and other such variables. Research shows that Native Americans, Hispanics, and African Americans are more likely to die from heart disease than other population groups. Koreans have the highest percentage of stomach cancer among other nationalities. More people living in the southeastern states die from stroke than in other parts of the country. Males suffer a much higher rate of deaths from auto accidents than do females. Why is this so? The answers may or may not be obvious and often involve relating the dependent variable (disease or health condition) to a number of possible independent or causal variables. While some ailments can usually be traced to a particular social group, for instance eating disorders among females, others are less apparent. For example, environmental pollution affects people differently irrespective of social group. What is apparent is that life expectancy among all groups and classes in the United States has historically been on the rise; however, the recent opioid crisis has had a downward impact on white, middle-aged males. Again, the question, why is this so?

MEDICINE IN THE UNITED STATES

We tend to think of medicine as pills and drugs. However, sociologically speaking, **medicine** refers to *the social institution that focuses on combating disease and improving health*. Medicine fits within the broader category of **health care**, which is *any activity intended to improve health*. If one joins a fitness club, alters their diet to include more nutritious foods, or even adopts a more positive attitude towards life, they are contributing to their overall health care as much as having regular check-ups with their physician or clinician.

Whereas countries around the world employ various systems for dealing with health issues, medicine in the United States is largely predicated on a direct fee system, meaning that the individual is financially responsible for his or her health care. However, most Americans are covered by some sort of insurance. Figures show that 56% of people in the United States have private insurance plans, about 20% are covered by **Medicaid**, which is *a government program that pays the health costs of low income people,* and around 16% have personal health plans including those obtained under the Affordable Care Act. Older people have **Medicare** coverage which is *the federal health insurance program for People who are 65 or older.* Medicare is offered as part of a person's social security package. Since insurance companies pay the bulk of the costs for health care, they were instrumental in the creation of **health maintenance**

© 2011 New York College of Health Professions

FIGURE 18.2. College of Health Professions, HHC Center Reception Room.

organizations (HMOs), *which are health insurance organizations to which subscribers pay a predetermined fee in return for a range of medical services.* The aim of HMOs of course was to minimize the costs that insurance companies pay to providers.

The mixed system of public and private health coverage in the United States has stimulated a lively political debate. Defenders of the free enterprise system claim that competition in the private sector with minimum government controls is the best way to keep down costs and provide top notch care. Others who point to the inefficiencies, inequalities, and expense of the present arrangement claim that a single-payer system, much along the lines of making Medicare more comprehensive would be more fair, efficient, and equitable. This would follow closely the kind of comprehensive health care programs that exist in many other countries.

DELIVERY OF HEALTH CARE SERVICES IN THE UNITED STATES

There are two approaches to the provision of medicine and health care which to some degree overlap. **Scientific medicine**, or *the science and art dealing with the maintenance of health and the prevention, alleviation, or cure of disease,*[1] has been the dominant form of delivery for well over a century, and in most cases has proven to

---

1   *Merriam-Webster*, s.v. "medicine," https://www.merriam-webster.com/dictionary/medicine.

be highly effective. The application of the scientific method in dealing with health issues has led to the centralization of medical practice in hospitals and clinics, resulting in a high degree of specialization. Since this approach is largely based on responding to a specific cause or symptom, scientific medicine has become drug oriented in its treatments. At the same time, it has fostered tight controls through the American Medical Association, along with insurance and drug companies and government regulatory agencies.

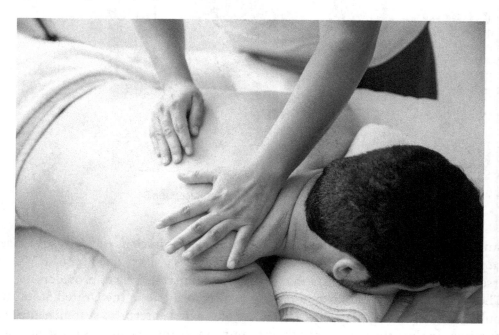

FIGURE 18.3. Holistic Massage Therapist.

The high cost and what some people consider the narrow focus of scientific medicine has led to the emergence of holistic medicine. So defined, **holistic medicine** is *a form of healing that considers the whole person—body, mind, spirit, and emotions in the quest for optimal health and wellness.*[2] Such treatments take account of a wide range of therapies that include naturopathy, homeopathy, acupuncture, the use of herbs, and often spiritual practices such as meditation, yoga, and tai chi. The purpose of holistic medicine is to consider the health needs of the individual and recommend appropriate treatment accordingly. There is also an emphasis on altering one's lifestyle in ways to promote better health. The effectiveness of holistic medicine in comparison to

2 "What is Holistic Medicine?" WebMD, June 2017, https://www.webmd.com/balance/guide/what-is-holistic-medicine#1.

scientific medicine is a matter of debate; however, it has widened the scope of treatment, offering greater choice for those in need of medical services.

THEORETICAL ANALYSIS

From the structural-functional perspective, health and medicine is about the performance of specific roles. There are generally three such categories. The ill person performs the sick role. This requires that such a person does everything they can to take care of themselves. This would involve staying home from work or missing classes, going to bed so as to get plenty of rest, and following the advice and direction of caretakers and healthcare personnel. The physician's role is to attend to the patient in an appropriate manner and prescribe palliative medicines or therapies. The support group role would be to make the patient as comfortable as possible and assume the responsibilities of the sick person while they are incapacitated. Clearly, the implication is that the performance of these roles would have the most beneficial or functional effect, whereas the failure to fulfill any or all of these roles would contribute to dysfunctionality.

The conflict model highlights institutional inequality. It assumes that there is an unequal access to health care due to the fact that a large number of people lack the means and resources to afford sufficient care. This is especially true in a society based on a direct fee system where individuals are responsible for the payment of medical services. Whereas by law everyone in the United States is required to be treated, the quality and extent of care depends upon one's resources. Estimates show that approximately thirty-three million Americans lack health insurance often due to low incomes or poverty.[3] Given that hospitals and clinics are largely private businesses, they operate according to the profit motive in much the same manner as other commercial organizations.

According to the interaction paradigm, health and illness are the products of subjective perceptions. What is a normal or abnormal medical condition? This is far from a clear-cut question and may vary according to place or situation. For instance, the diagnosis of a chest pain in one society may result in a diagnosis that is significantly different from how it might be seen in another society. Even though physicians use a similar method in identifying an ailment, their treatment may be conditioned by cultural factors.

By the same token, one's perception of illness may be influenced by non-medical factors. If you were looking forward to going to a party or some fun event but were

---

3 Anna Maria Barry-Jester and Ben Casselman, "33 Million Americans Still Don't Have Health Insurance," FiveThirtyEight, September 28, 2015, https://fivethirtyeight.com/features/33-million-americans-still-dont-have-health-insurance/.

experiencing a slight temperature or had a mild sore throat, you might be willing to overlook these symptoms and go ahead with your plans. Conversely, if you were faced with an exam you hadn't prepared for, you would perhaps see these symptoms as a more serious illness and chose to stay in bed and take a make-up exam later. Essentially, the matter of your illness would be determined by the context of your circumstances, rather than your physical condition.

AGING

The study of aging and the elderly in a society is called **gerontology**. Gerontologists look at many aspects of the aging process including biological changes resulting from wear and tear and the dysfunctions of the body, changes in one's psychological state of mind, and the impact of cultural and social influences on aging. For example, as people get older they require more support services. At the same time, retirement may lead to the loss of income, resulting sometimes in anxiety and financial hardship. However, over a number of decades the number of older people in poverty has decreased. Between 1960 and 1995, the official poverty rate of those aged sixty-five and above fell from thirty-five percent to *ten* percent, and research has documented similarly steep declines dating back to at least 1939.[4]

Furthermore, retirement leads to many lifestyle changes. While these changes may be challenging for some, there is evidence that retirees who enter into new roles and responsibilities often have longer and happier lives than those who fall into sedentary modes of living. It should be noted that voluntary organizations are in many cases staffed by older people.

It is no secret that the United States is an aging society evidenced by a decline in the birth rate and increased life expectancy. As proportionally more people enter old age, a greater number of resources, particularly medical resources, will be required for their use and care. According to 2016 figures, the number of Americans ages sixty-five and older is projected to more than double from forty-six million today to over ninety-eight million by 2060, and the sixty-five-and-older age group's share of the total population will rise to nearly twenty-four percent from fifteen percent.[5] This corresponds to a greater or lesser degree with the aging patterns in other western countries.

---

4   "Social Security and Elderly Poverty," National Bureau of Economic Research, http://www.nber.org/aginghealth/summer04/w10466.html.

5   "Fact Sheet: Aging in the United States," Population Reference Bureau, January 13, 2016, https://www.prb.org/aging-unitedstates-fact-sheet/.

DEATH AND DYING

Death, the last stage in the life cycle, would appear to be an obvious occurrence. However, if we ask the question, who or what dies, the answer is more problematic. The physical body dies of course and disintegrates but what about the soul and the levels of consciousness of the deceased person? Accepting the reality of reincarnation, it is clear that part of oneself passes from one life to another. Beyond a recognition of this fact, nothing more needs to be said.

Death and dying over past centuries was viewed far differently than that of today. Generally, death was an ever-present fact of life due to its frequency. In 19th century America, the average life expectancy for men was about 36 years and for women about 38 years. Poor nutrition, the lack of medical resources, the invasiveness of pandemic diseases, plus strenuous overwork, not to mention high incidences of child mortality were obvious causes of an early death rate. Much of this has changed. In 2010 life expectancy for men was seventy-seven years and for women eighty-three years! Between 2000 and 2010, the life expectancy for both sexes increased by over two years.

Death, like most things in life, is a process. In her 1969 book *Death and Dying*, psychiatrist Elisabeth Kübler-Ross identified five stages of dying categorized as denial, anger, bargaining, depression, and acceptance. Naturally, these stages would not apply when death was sudden or unexpected. Critics have also claimed that there is a lack of empirical evidence to support this five-stage process.[6] Moreover, persons and loved ones undergoing the activity of dying may skip some or all of these steps. Also, it could be said that one's approach to death is predicated on their level of consciousness, and thereby may not evoke a similar response. Over the past several decades, the hospice movement has expanded. **Hospice** *provides palliative care for those terminally or seriously ill, helps alleviate pain, and attends to their emotional and spiritual needs.*

While Americans often describe the US health care system as the best in the world, a report from the Commonwealth Fund suggests that "the U.S. health care system ranks last among 11 high-income countries. The country leads the world in health care spending, but its residents are sicker and more likely to die of preventable conditions than those in other wealthy countries."[7] Consequently, the need to provide better health care for an aging population at a more reasonable cost will be a major national priority.

---

6   David P. Feldman, "Why the Five Stages of Grief Are Wrong," *Psychology Today*, July 7, 2017, https://www.psychologytoday.com/us/blog/supersurvivors/201707/why-the-five-stages-grief-are-wrong.

7   Eric C. Schneider and David Squires, "From Last to First — Could the U.S. Health Care System Become the Best in the World?" The Commonwealth Fund, July 17, 2017, https://www.commonwealthfund.org/publications/journal-article/2017/jul/last-first-could-us-health-care-system-become-best-world.

STUDY QUESTIONS

1. Suggest some reasons why patterns of health are distinctive with respect to race, ethnicity, and gender? Give specific examples to support your answer.
2. Discuss the relative merits of a public health system (government run health care programs) as opposed to a private or direct fee system. What are the strengths and weaknesses of both approaches?
3. Discuss the challenges that an aging population will force on American society in the coming years.

Figure Credits

UNIT V

Transition to a New Age

FOR THOSE OF us who were born within the past few generations, it is difficult to comprehend the vast changes that have taken place in less than a century. The pace of change has quickened remarkably through the rapid acceleration of technology as we move from an industrial to a post-modern, or information-based, society. The vast increase in population has put pressure on existing institutions, fostering readjustments and dysfunctions. Societal changes and the expansion of education have affected human consciousness in ways that seem imperceptible. As more and more people develop the capacity to think, and are less swayed by demagogues and outside pressures, they are beginning to see the world in a different light. Greater toleration and the acceptance of cultures and peoples who are different are important aspects of this shift in consciousness.

Conversely, at the same time, the pressure of change has brought to the surface ancient hatreds, suspicions, and conflicts that are presently being played out on the world stage. Constant warfare, upheavals, and terrorism are ever-present, invoking fears and a pervasive climate of pessimism. One might also argue that humanity is confronted with a spiritual crisis, meaning an inability to think beyond a limiting framework of understanding. What this portends for the future is hard to say, but if sociology is to be effective it must help us to understand the dynamic pressures and forces that condition the world in which we live, move, and have our being.

CHAPTER NINETEEN

Demography, Urbanization, & the Natural Environment

IN LESOTHO, a small landlocked kingdom in southern Africa, it has been estimated that with a population of 2.6 million, over half of the people in that country face starvation due in part to the lingering impact of drought. Lesotho was not alone as similar conditions and subsequent consequences can be found in seventeen other African nations. Persistent dry weather, however, is not the fundamental cause of this problem. It is overpopulation. Throughout Africa, across parts of Asia and certain other places in the world, the population has been expanding precipitously to the point where local food sources cannot support this growth. Despite foreign aid and attempts at development in accordance with modernization theory, absolute poverty remains a critical issue in Lesotho and elsewhere. Hence, questions relating to the relationship between population and resources remain at the heart of the severe economic and social problems that face humanity today.

BASIC DEMOGRAPHIC CONCEPTS

The study of human population is called **demography**. Population composition and growth is defined by certain basic concepts, which are fertility, mortality, and migration. **Fertility** is *the rate of births to women of childbearing age*. Fertility differs from **fecundity**, which is defined as *the potential for reproduction*. The crude birth rate is calculated by dividing the number of births in a given society by the total population times one thousand.

Mortality relates to *the incidence of death in a particular population*. Likewise, the crude death rate is determined by the number of deaths per year divided by the total population multiplied by one thousand. The infant mortality rate would be figured by the same calculation for children under one year of age.

Migration refers to *the movement of people into or out of a society*, usually on a permanent or semi-permanent basis. To calculate the rate of population growth, one would subtract the number of deaths from those of births (usually higher), which would give the natural growth rate. By adding or subtracting the rate of migration (whichever was greater), one could then determine the total population growth. Let us assume, for example, that in a given society the crude birth rate was 10,000 and the crude death rate was 8,500. By subtracting the latter from the former we would find that the natural growth rate was 1,500. If over the same year 2,000 people migrated into this society, the total population growth would be 3,500.

THEORIES OF POPULATION GROWTH

Malthusian Theory

The Reverend Thomas Malthus who lived in England between 1766 and 1834 developed a theory of population that has had wide application. Essentially what Malthus argued was that in a given society, the rate of population over time would rise geometrically (at a rate of 1,2,4,8,16,32,64, etc.) whereas life sustaining resources (food supply) could only grow arithmetically (at a rate of 1,2,3,4,5,6, etc.). Sooner or later population increase would outstrip the available food sources leading to a demographic catastrophe. Famine, widespread disease, war or some other calamity resulting from overpopulation constituted what Malthus called positive checks. These sorts of checks largely affected pre-industrial societies where there were few artificial population controls. The country of Lesotho (mentioned earlier) offers a good example of the working out of Malthusian theory. Malthus referred to population control through various birth control methods, such as condoms, birth control pills, and other such devices as preventive checks. Being a rather puritanical minister, Malthus preferred abstinence as the best form of birth control but he was pessimistic that it would be effective. Research and subsequent experience has substantiated his fears.

Demographic Transition Theory

A more modern theory of population change is **demographic transition theory**. It is a model used to represent the movement of high birth and death rates to low birth and death rates as a country develops from a pre-industrial to an industrialized economic system.[1] This transition is divided into three stages. During the first or pre-industrial stage, the birth rate is high, but so is the death rate due to accelerated rates of infant mortality, limiting the capacity for reproduction. In a large family of eight children,

---

1   Ashley Crossman, "What Is the Demographic Transition Model?" ThoughtCo., March 6, 2017, https://www.thoughtco.com/demographic-transition-definition-3026248.

for instance, six children may die and often did so before they were old enough to marry and start families of their own.

During the second phase, the population rapidly increases due to a decline in the death rate. The reasons for this decline remain unclear but changes in diet, better medical care, or even a more positive outlook on life may be factors. At any rate, more children are living longer and so are able to produce more offspring. Likewise, the birth rate remains high and life expectancy increases. This transition phase coincides with rapid economic growth through increased trade, more and better transportation networks, and a host of other factors.

FIGURE 19.1. Crowd.

The third phase of population transition occurs when a society has become more economically mature. At this point, the death rate stabilizes and the birth rate decreases. Hence, the natural growth rate declines as the gap between the birth and death rate narrows. Whereas during the first phase, the population was primarily youthful, by the time a society reaches the third stage it is aging. Whereas the timeframe for these stages varies considerably from one society to another, it does follow a progressive pattern. It could be said that demographic transition theory has some correlation to modernization theory, whereas Malthusian theory, which is characteristic of a continuous cycle of poverty, fits more conveniently with dependency theory.

GLOBAL POPULATION PATTERNS

The demographics of world population could largely be explained by drawing a line around the center of the planet. Generally speaking, those countries to the north of the line would be characterized by low or steady population growth in accordance with the third stage of demographic transition, whereas those countries to the south would be undergoing high growth rates in line with the second stage.

Comparative populations can be illustrated through age-ascending population pyramids. The data shows that poorer nations have a predominately youthful population which is illustrated by a broad base at the bottom of the pyramid, becoming increasingly narrow as it ascends through older age groups. The pyramid for richer nations is quite different. The bottom of the pyramid is relatively thin, becoming bulkier towards the middle, and thin again near the top. The pyramid for richer nations, in terms of millions of people, is far smaller than that for poorer nations. In both cases, there are slightly more females than males.

Since population is one of those social statistics that can be projected into the future with a relative degree of accuracy, scholars have been able to put forth a number of scenarios. With the global population standing at around 7.6 billion, some estimates propose that by 2030 the number of inhabitants on earth will rise to 8.5 billion, further to 9.7 billion by 2050, and levelling off to 11.2 billion by 2100.[2] These figures, of course, are subject to fluctuation by any number of variables. Some researchers have suggested that the maximum food resources of the planet; are only sufficient to feed 10 billion people.[3] While this projection is certainly debatable, it does point to a Malthusian scenario that has sobering possibilities. This is all the more so since the bulk of the projected rise in population will come from poor countries.

Urbanization

Gradual population growth over the centuries has led to **urbanization**, which is *the concentration of humanity into cities*. At first, dating back to the ancient world, cities were small settlements often built around temples. As societies became more complex, the function and size of towns and cities grew accordingly. The medieval city, for instance, was a compact unit often surrounded by a wall containing shops, churches, small cottage industries, and private dwellings. With the coming of the Industrial Revolution, cities greatly expanded as many people migrated from rural areas to work in factories and mills. Industrialization produced more jobs and statuses that further expanded the scope and range of the urban region.

---

2   Max Roser and Esteban Ortiz-Ospina, "World Population Growth," Our World in Data, updated April 2017, https://ourworldindata.org/world-population-growth.

3   Natalie Wolchover, "How Many People Can Earth Support?" Live Science, October 11, 2011, https://www.livescience.com/16493-people-planet-earth-support.html.

FIGURE 19.2. Urban Los Angeles.

As population continues to expand, it is estimated that sixty-eight percent of the world's population will live in urban areas by the year 2050, up from fifty-five percent at present according to a United Nations report.[4] There has also been a geographic shift. In 1950, five of the ten largest cities in the world were in Europe and the United States. By the year 2018, no western city was in the top ten. The largest city in the world is Shanghai with a population of 24.2 million followed closely by Beijing with 21.5 million. Both these cities are in China, which is the world's largest country with close to 1.4 billion people.

Modern Urban Patterns

The modern city has evolved new patterns that are significantly different from the centralized industrial city of the past that contained a business district at the core with concentric rings of commercial enterprises and dwellings spreading outwards. One of modern urban development has been the decline of city centers, as people have become more mobile (thanks to the automobile), coupled with the expansion of suburbs. This trend has been reversed somewhat in recent years due to the gentrification of downtown areas through the building of expensive homes, high end rental properties, and upscale shops and restaurants.

With the expansion of suburbs, the post-industrial city has been characterized by urban sprawl, which includes mile after mile of shopping centers, service industries, and neighborhood communities. This has been especially true of Sunbelt cities like Houston and Phoenix among others. Concomitant with urban sprawl is the emergence of **edge cities**, which are *relatively large urban areas situated on the outskirts of a city, typically beside a major interstate highway or thoroughfare.* The addition of suburbs and edge cities has witnessed the rise of **metropolitan statistical areas** (MSAs), *which are geographical regions with a relatively high population density at its core and close economic ties throughout the area.*[5] The largest MSA in the United States is the New York-New Jersey metropolitan region containing 20.1 million people.

Cities are essentially layers of human activity seen as a series of overlaid maps. **Urban ecology** refers to the scientific study of the relation of living organisms with

---

4   "2018 Revision of World Urbanization Prospects," United Nations, May 16, 2018, https://www.un.org/development/desa/publications/2018-revision-of-world-urbanization-prospects.html.

5   "Metropolitan Statistical Area (MSA)," Investopedia, https://www.investopedia.com/terms/m/msa.asp.

each other and their surroundings in the context of an urban environment.[6] Within this context, one would look for connections between the economic, political, and social dimensions of a city and how the parts interact with one-another. Sociologist Robert Park used his experience as a beat reporter in Chicago in the early part of the last century to map out the city as ecosystems of human behavior patterns that determined the moral and social life of the region. Similarly, the concept of urban political economy looks at how economic factors are shaped by local state and political institutions as they affect urban areas.[7] Put another way, the city is viewed as a composite of property arrangements and commodities that condition the way cities function.

With the expansion and improvement of transportation systems along with modern technological developments such as the Internet, social media, and other such mediums of communication, the degree of separation between urban and rural regions has been greatly minimized. Writing at a time when rural existence was provincial, slow, and relatively unstimulating, Karl Marx referred to "the idiocy of rural life." This statement today would no longer be true.

ENVIRONMENT AND SOCIETY

The explosion of population over the past half-century has contributed to issues relating to the health of the natural environment. Whereas for many centuries, people paid little heed to the well-being of the planet, serious concerns are now expressed as to whether the natural environment can support a sustainable future. **Natural environment** refers to *the earth's surface and atmosphere including living organisms, air, water, soil, and other resources necessary to sustain life.*

Scientists who engage in *the study of the interaction between living organisms and the natural environment* known as **ecology** have come to view the environment as a vast **ecosystem** composed of the interaction of all living organisms in their natural habitat. The implication is that damage to one part of the ecosystem will adversely affect other parts of the system since all spheres of life are interconnected. One of the formulas used to assess environmental impact is the relationship between pollution, the degree of affluence within a society, and levels of technology (I=PAT).

The impact on the natural environment can essentially be traced back to the consequences of human behavior. Even though nature, like all things, moves according to cycles, the extremes are man-made. **Global warming** is defined as *an increase in the earth's average temperature that causes corresponding changes in climate.* The heating

---

6 "Urban Forestry," Indiana University, winter 2017, https://urbanforestry.indiana.edu/doc/publications/2016-iaa.pdf.

7 "Urban Political Economy," IResearchNet.com, http://sociology.iresearchnet.com/urban-sociology/urban-political-economy/.

of the atmosphere due primarily to the release of pollutants and carbon dioxide, largely as a by-product of industrial processes, coupled with the destruction of the rain forests, has resulted in a number of problems. The warming of oceans, which has accelerated since the mid-1970s, has caused erratic and extreme weather patterns such as excessive floods, hurricanes, and melting of the polar icecaps. Global warming is also a major factor behind declining biodiversity. The dire state of global warming has led politicians and scientists to call for a Green New Deal, requiring vast expenditures to meet environmental challenges. Ultimately, global cooperation and international treaties will need to be followed to further prevent future disasters and save the planet.

FIGURE 19.3. Satellite View of Hurricane Katrina.

The other primary factor affecting the environment has resulted from the exponential increase in population and the stress of economic growth that has contributed to water and air pollution, untold tons of solid waste, and pressure on available resources. Perhaps the greatest challenge facing humanity is how to square the need for a sustainable future, and thus restore some degree of balance in the natural environment, with the insatiable demands for more products and a better lifestyle spurred on by capitalism. The question of how to achieve limits to growth will likely haunt nations and peoples for years to come.

STUDY QUESTIONS

1. In what ways do population trends in the world today reflect both Malthusian Theory and Demographic Transition Theory?
2. Given the environmental crisis we face today, is it possible to reconcile the desire for economic growth and a concern to protect the environment? Give clear evidence to support your argument.
3. Discuss some of the ways that global economic patterns might support dependency theory (chapter 15).

Figure Credits

Fig. 19.1: Copyright © 2015 Depositphotos/zhudifeng.
Fig. 19.2: Copyright © 2018 Depositphotos/cboswell.
Fig. 19.3: Source: https://commons.wikimedia.org/wiki/File:Katrina1615z-050829-1kg12.jpg.

CHAPTER TWENTY

Collective Behavior—War, Revolution, and Terrorism

IN HIS BOOK, *The Revolt of the Masses* published in 1930, the Spanish philosopher José Ortega y Gasset argued that the most significant development in the modern world was the rise of what he called mass man. The emergence of mass man was not only a statistical phenomenon due to rapid population growth in Europe, but a challenge to the western system of values that had existed for centuries. Accordingly, the masses were detached from the past, lacking purpose or any sense of direction, yet self-satisfied and morally ambiguous. While Ortega's assessment of the social world is significantly different than that of today, his characterization of mass man, or average man is still relevant even though large segments of the population have evolved in consciousness to the point where they are more civilized, somewhat cultured, and live useful lives often devoted to helping others. It is this gap in consciousness, coupled with widening social and economic cleavages, that is at the root of many of the world's conflicts and problems. To understand more fully the nature of mass society and the dynamics of war, revolution, and terrorism, we need to probe these issues further, commencing with an examination of collective behavior.

COLLECTIVE BEHAVIOR

Collective Behavior is defined as *the unified activity involving a large number of people whether organized or not.* While this definition is sufficiently vague, there are certain characteristics that govern all forms of mass behavior. First of all, it is diverse. Collective behavior is commonplace throughout human society whether planned or loosely formed. Secondly, it is often hard to explain. Many crowds and groups come together and disperse without any clear impetus, although this would not apply to a planned activity such as a crowd at a football game. Thirdly, collective behavior is usually transitory. Common to all forms of group activity is that it is of limited duration to a greater or lesser degree.

As covered in part in chapter six, there are various types of collective behavior. Two of the most common forms are an aggregate and a crowd. An aggregate is a large number of people who engage in minimal interaction in the absence of well-defined conventional norms. An example would be a group of people waiting at a bus stop. In such a gathering, people would most likely occupy a similar space without interacting or even noticing those standing nearby. A crowd consists of a temporary gathering of people who share a common focus of attention and who influence one another. A group of people at a rock concert, sporting event, or a church congregation would clearly fit the definition of a crowd. A crowd is a social fact insofar as it has an objective reality beyond the individuals within the group, which lends itself to certain social patterns.

FIGURE 20.1. Rally in Grand Army Plaza After Death of George Floyd.

Consequently, the assemblage of a large number of people often opens the door for suggestive behavior. A chant that is picked up by others or the wave at a football match are indicative of the sensitivity of crowds to various types of stimuli.

Crowds may be active or passive. When an emotionally charged crowd responds to a precipitating event or situation, it may lead to a mob or riot. A **mob** can have several meanings but is usually defined as *a disorderly crowd that may have a violent or destructive intent*. Mobs often direct their anger at some particular target or goal. The lynching of African Americans by a mob in the South during the period of apartheid in the United States is one clear example. Mob activity can lead to a **riot**, which is *a social eruption that is highly emotional, violent, and often undirected*. Riots usually lead to a complete breakdown of law and order and may last for an extended period of time. The race riots that took place in Detroit and Newark, NJ in 1967 lasted five days with considerable loss of life and destruction of property.

Perhaps the best explanation of mob activity and riot is **contagion theory**. *This theory put forward by the French sociologist Gustave Le Bon argues that such riotous events are eruptions of irrational behavior that draw in people who might otherwise not be a party to these happenings*. In response to the apparent normlessness of contagion theory, some sociologists have posited **emergent-norm theory**, which contends that *social disruptions involve the rejection of one set of norms for another set of norms*. Activities that often occur during a riot, such as looting stores for instance, would be seen in this context as normative. Thus, lawlessness has its own set of norms provided that law violation becomes for its duration the dominant mode of social behavior.

COMMONPLACE PATTERNS THAT INFLUENCE COLLECTIVE BEHAVIOR

Rumor and Gossip

Information that conditions group behavior is often spread by word of mouth or through various communication media. A common form of often false information dissemination is **rumor**, which is *circulating unconfirmed information that is spread informally*. Rumors often thrive in a climate of uncertainty. For example, if a company starts laying off some staff, a rumor may take form suggesting that the organization is about to close down, which was not the case. By the same token, rumors are often unstable. Stories that are passed along from person to person tend to become embellished so that the rumor becomes far different, and usually much more exaggerated, than what it was originally. Finally, rumors are difficult to stop. Even when there is sufficient evidence to the contrary, people are more likely to accept the rumor than the truth especially if it is sensational and conforms to one's preconceived biases. The widespread use of social media has added fuel to the fire of rumor, thus creating a serious problem as to the validity of facts and transmitted information when confronted with "fake news."

Whereas, generally speaking, rumor relates to any unconfirmed information that is transmitted, **gossip** is *idle talk or rumor, especially about the personal or private affairs of others*. The curious and pervasive interest that many people entertain regarding the private lives and behavior of acquaintances, friends, and co-workers gives vent to a lot of gossip. Media gossip about the lives of the rich and famous plays upon mass desire

FIGURE 20.2. The Harvard–Yale Game. College Sports as a Popular Form of Collective Behavior.

to devour and share sensational stories that may mirror one's own circumstances and experiences.

Fashion and Fads

Fashions and fads often shape the momentary interests of the mass of people. **Fashion** refers to *a popular social pattern or style favored by a large group of people at any particular time*. It is especially noticeable with respect to such things as clothing, footwear, lifestyle, accessories, makeup, hairstyle, and body adornment. Fashion is a distinctive and often constant trend in the style in which people present themselves. The popularity of tattoos is one such example, so are particular films, video games and other forms of popular entertainment. According to the Consumer Insight Service, ninety-eight percent of adults between the ages of eighteen and twenty-four use social media, which speaks to a fashion that has changed how young people communicate and spend their time.

Fads are *an intense and widely shared enthusiasm for something, especially one that is short-lived and without basis in the object's qualities, referred to as a craze.*[1] Back in the 1960s, hula hoops were a popular fad and so was streaking (running through public places naked). A fad may be restricted to a particular subculture or have a brief acceptance across a broader population. The constant emergence and disappearance of fashions and fads speaks to the widespread and complex nature of social patterns that capture our attention for the moment and then are forgotten.

Public Opinion and Propaganda

It is no mystery that public opinion is largely shaped by propaganda. **Public opinion** is defined as *the collective opinion of many people on some problem or issue.* **Propaganda** is *information, especially of a biased or misleading nature, used to promote or publicize a particular product, political cause or point of view.*[2] Put together, these two terms characterize the problem of how people think about the world in which they live. As every politician knows, public opinion is constantly changing so what people think is important today fades away when another matter of concern arises. For instance, many people opposed the Affordable Care Act passed under the Obama administration until they realized that it could benefit them.

Propaganda is often used to sway public opinion to support or oppose an idea, law, or policy. At its best, propaganda may serve as a helpful source of information. At its worst, it can misinform, distort, or over-simplify an issue. British Prime Minister Winston Churchill's quote that "the best argument against democracy is a five-minute conversation with the average voter" was not intended to be unkind. Rather he was pointing to the fact that in a mass democratic society where in theory the people rule, a general lack of interest in political concerns, coupled with the effect of propaganda in shaping public opinion can cause a representative form of government to be dysfunctional.

SOCIAL MOVEMENTS

The tension between forces of change and those of reaction has precipitated the emergence of social movements. A **social movement** is *a group of diffusely organized people or organizations striving toward a common goal relating to human society that encourages or discourages social change.* Social movements often go through stages of emergence, coalescence, bureaucratization, and decline. In other words, social movements generally commence around a cause or matter to be fixed, then pull in people or groups that are sympathetic to that cause. As it becomes more complex, the movement develops a set

---

1 Karol Janicki, *Language Misconceived: Arguing for Applied Cognitive Sociolinguistics* (Routledge, 2014), 8.

2 Oxford Living Dictionaries, s.v. "propaganda," https://en.oxforddictionaries.com/definition/propaganda.

of rules, norms, and organizational structure, and finally it declines after having achieved its goals, or more often when internal or external pressures cause it to disperse or collapse. The civil rights movement in the United States followed such a pattern. Having achieved its goal of ending racial segregation, it fragmented when confronted with more intractable problems such as combating economic and social injustice.

FIGURE 20.3. Iraq–Dusk.

There are a number of theories that help to explain social movements. In a mass society, **relative deprivation theory** *explains the gap that develops between those who have sufficient resources and those lacking these resources.* When the "have nots" become conscious of this disparity and believe that they should have a larger piece of the pie, then they are motivated, largely through illegal or unconventional means to acquire more power or resources. This often comes about through creating a social movement. **Mass society theory** posits that *people who are alienated, powerless or otherwise discon-nected in a society will gravitate to movements that promise hope, certainty, and a sense of belonging.* The now-vanquished Islamic State of Iraq and the Levant, known as the Islamic State and labelled a terrorist organization, conformed to this theory insofar as it attracted many marginalized people from various countries who were alienated and attracted to its fundamentalist message of certainty and comradeship. Finally, **resource mobilization theory** maintains that *an organized social movement will only* *come about if the necessary resources are available.* Such resources might include money, sufficient leadership, people with skills, communication networks, and many other things. Information technologies have greatly enhanced the ability of social movements to expand and function through their ability to network, mobilize, and spread vital information. These theories offer a partial explanation for the incidences of war, revolution, and terrorism that are so prevalent at this time.

WAR, REVOLUTION, AND TERRORISM

Wars have occurred with such frequency and regularity throughout history that they are assumed to be normative. **War** is *a state of armed conflict between different nations, states, or factions within a nation-state, as in the case of a civil war.* While there are multiple reasons for why wars start such as border disputes, the assertion of national pride, or a desire to dominate other people or a region, they almost always involve planned operations involving state direction and military personnel. While we often think that the alternative to war is peace, it is in fact change. When nations of societies become crystalized, the forces of evolution generate conflict that eventually leads to military conflict. Wars can be fought on different planes. National pride, an emotional response, has frequently precipitated armed conflict, and so has ideology. The Cold War between the United States and the Soviet Union was one such example. Wars today are less about winning or losing and often result in stalemate over a number of years. Resource mobilization theory helps to explain the basis for war since wars are costly and require vast resources of men, weaponry, money, and loads of other materials.

Since World War II, the United States has fought in fourteen major wars and numerous brush fire wars. The cost of war is high. According to the Stockholm International Peace Research Institute,[3] the United States spent more money on its military ($610 billion in 2017) than the next seven countries with large military budgets ($578 billion). Much of this money is funneled into large corporations such as Lockheed Martin, Raytheon, and General Dynamics Corporation in the form of government contracts to produce war materials. Thus, it can be said that war is good for business.

Like war, there have been many political revolutions over the course of time. A **political revolution** is defined as *the overthrow of a political system in order to establish another system.* Whereas wars are between nations and groups, revolutions occur between those holding power and armed resistors within a country. Revolutions can

---

3 "Global military spending remains high at $1.7 trillion," Stockholm International Peace Research Institute, May 2, 2018, https://www.sipri.org/media/press-release/2018/global-military-spending-remains-high-17-trillion.

be explained in part by relative deprivation theory since oppressed people are more likely to revolt if they perceive that their lives could be better under a new regime. This in itself would not be a sufficient explanation since revolutions often occur after a long period of cruel or unjust mismanagement by a domineering government or class. Thus, the regime in power loses its legitimacy and conflict ensues. Karl Marx argued that the overthrow of the bourgeoisie by the proletariat would come about as a result of the complete domination of the capitalist system and the crushing of the working class, which had no other choice.

Political, economic, and social upheaval in various parts of the world have been conducive to the rise of terrorism. **Terrorism** is defined as *the unlawful use of violence and intimidation, especially against civilians, in the pursuit of political aims.*[4] As such, it is a political strategy often used to create fear and chaos to meet certain demands or force change. Terrorism is also intended to create **mass hysteria**, which is *dispersed collective behavior in which people react out of fear or panic to a real, imagined, or manufactured event.* The threat of terrorism may be used as an ideological weapon to create a sense of imminent danger. While acts of terrorism overall are real, they tend to be isolated. In 2016, according to US State Department statistics,[5] there were 11,072 terrorist attacks around the world, mostly in regions of sectarian conflict including Iraq, Afghanistan, Syria, Nigeria, and Pakistan. In the United States, the chances of suffering a terrorist attack are extremely slight, less than one in twenty million. According to the National Consortium for the Study of Terrorism and Responses to Terrorism (START), there were 9,600 terrorist attacks around the world in 2018 which killed more than 22,960 people. 2018 was the fourth consecutive year of decline in global terrorism that reached a peak in 2014 with 17,000 attacks and more than 45,000 deaths.

While the United States has been largely immune from global terrorism, according to CBS News there were more mass shootings than days of the year in this country in 2019. By the end of the year, there were 417 mass shootings, based on data from the non-profit Gun Violence Archive (GVA). A **mass shooting** is defined as *any incident in which at least 4 people are shot."* At the height of the great Depression in 1933, President Franklin D. Roosevelt in his first inaugural address remarked "we have nothing to fear but fear itself." That statement is apt today with regard to the fear of domestic terrorism.

---

4   Oxford Living Dictionaries, s.v. "terrorism," https://en.oxforddictionaries.com/definition/terrorism.

5   "Annex of Statistical Information: Country Reports on Terrorism 2016," National Consortium for the Study of Terrorism and Responses to Terrorism, July 2017, https://www.state.gov/documents/organization/272485.pdf.

STUDY QUESTIONS

1. Could it be said that all news is propaganda? How can one discern the difference between an informed opinion and "fake news"?
2. In terms of social movements, discuss Resource Mobilization Theory, Mass Society Theory, and Resource Mobilization Theory. How do each of these theories relate to particular forms of conflict?
3. Discuss some of the ways fashion and fads gain traction. Why do certain social patterns invoke mass appeal, while others fail to get widespread recognition? Give specific examples.

CPSIA information can be obtained
at www.ICGtesting.com
Printed in the USA
LVHW061948110123
736877LV00002B/13

9 781516 538928